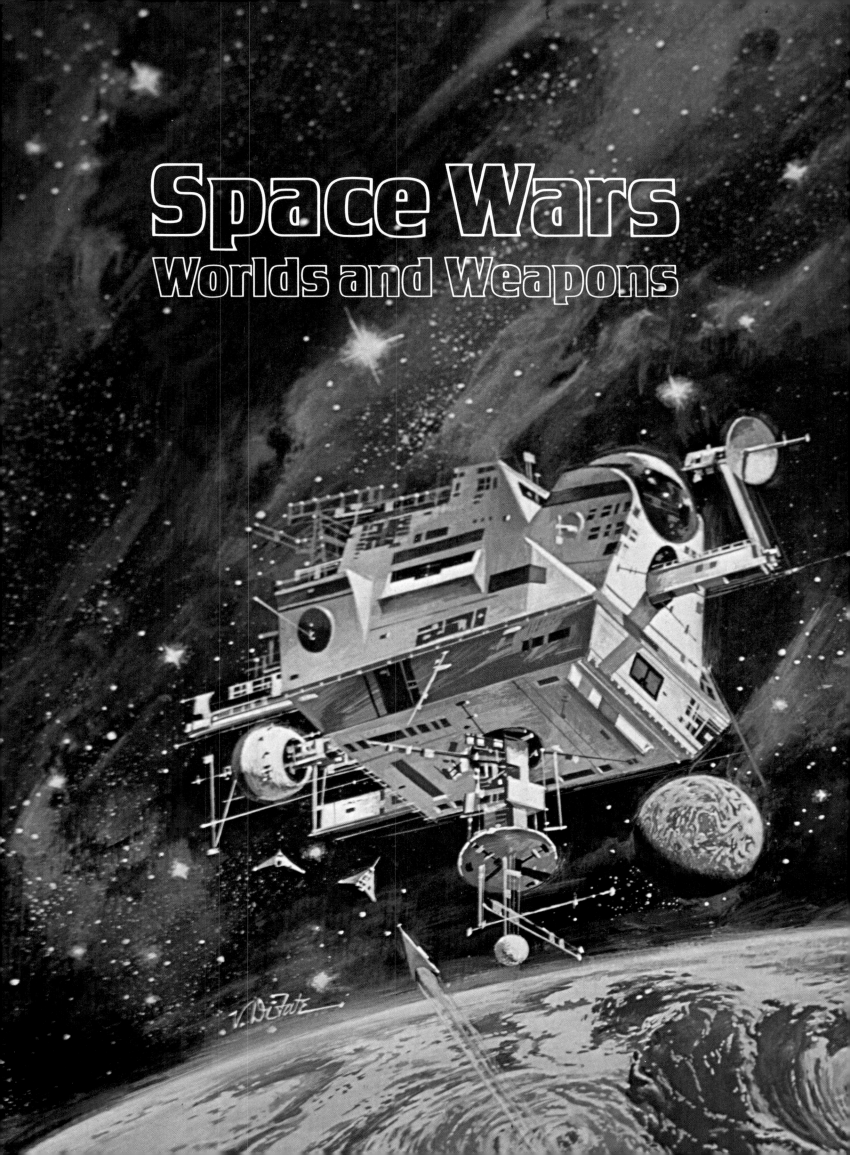

Space Wars
Worlds and Weapons

Space Wars
Worlds and Weapons

by Steven Eisler
Foreword by Chris Foss

CRESCENT
BOOKS
New York

First English edition published in 1979
by Octopus Books Limited
59 Grosvenor Street London W1

© MCMLXXIX Octopus Books Limited
Library of Congress Catalog Card Number 78/21588

This edition is published by Crescent Books,
a division of Crown Publishers, Inc.

Library of Congress Cataloging in Publication Data

Eisler, Steven.
Space Wars.

1. Science fiction – Illustrations. I. Title.
NC961.7.S34E37 1979   741.64   78-21588
ISBN 0-517-27344-6

Printed in Hong Kong

Contents

Foreword

This is a fascinating collection of futuristic visualisations
by various artists. Personally I take a rather pragmatic view
towards future developments. Depressingly perhaps, so many
artists see a future of wars and aggressive territorial
conflagrations – not unnaturally because, for some reason, so
many people see space warships as vividly coloured with
outrageous lines. Could it be conceivable that as the
colonisation of space takes place civilisations will inevitably
have to unite against the common foe – space itself! There are
fearsome distances to conquer – within you will find
descriptions of drive-systems designed to traverse the cosmos.
Isolated planets and asteroids will be of little commercial
value but possibly provide settlements for the generations of
constant travellers that future technology will generate.

What is interesting about this book is that so many artists
have been able to escape the obvious inspiration provided by
modern industrial and social developments. In here are
strange cities and alien galaxies, far from the realms of
current knowledge, yet suprisingly real such is the conviction
of the painter. Timeless Marie Celestes negotiate galactic
corridors, cognisant of their destination but not
acknowledging their past. There are meticulous conceptual
designs and flamboyant realisations. There is beauty, and of
course ugliness. We all have our personal oddysees and
perhaps in here you will find something to influence your own
passage through time.

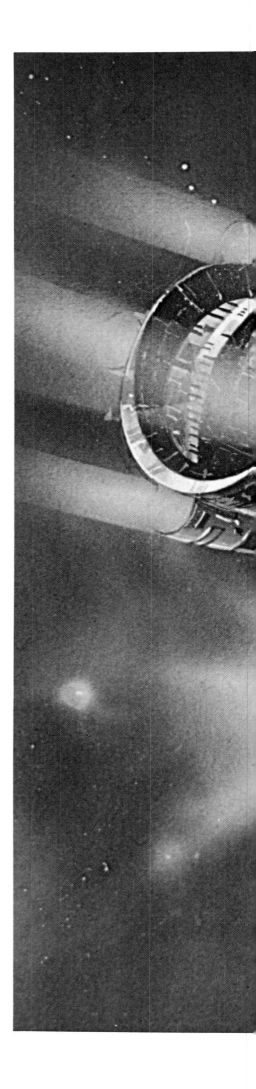

Space Vehicles

'. . . the transport factor connecting solar systems and universes'

However you call it—star ship, rocket ship, space machine—the space ship is the foremost, some would say the ultimate, sf symbol. If science fiction is all about other worlds, then the space ship is a part of that other-worldliness, connecting solar systems and universes . . . the public transport factor. If science fiction is all about the future, then the space ship is a part of that future, a mark of the bigger and greater technological capability of man's descendents. Of all the machine heroes of science fiction, only the robot is more heroic than the space ship, and like the robot, the space ship has often been both central idea and central character.

Several pre-Victorian woodcuts show man's first attempts to fly to the moon: huge, wooden-hulled galleons sail serenely between planets, their sails full blown before, one presumes, the solar wind. Cyrano de Bergerac's flying chariot, in which he made his *Voyage dans la Lune*, utilised the energy of the sun to draw up the dew for motive power. Both early romantic visions may seem ludicrous, but a certain sort of full circle was achieved in the modern fiction with the realisation that there *is* a wind between the worlds, the solar wind, the power of the photon. Sunjammers now frequently appear in sf, space ships of a weird and wonderful form, for they are literally blown through space by light pressure impinging on a vast solar sail. Arthur Clarke's Sunjammer has 50 million square feet of sail, connected to a tiny space capsule by over a hundred miles of rigging; the sail is no more substantial than a soap bubble, and made of aluminised plastic. Larry Niven and Jerry Pournelle's 'Crazy Eddie Probe'

Quirinian faxTime Drive Monitoring Station *With the peace and prosperity that accompanied the Third Empire—the Quirinian Empire —time research ultimately made the breakthrough and a few select timegates were permanently established in the galaxy. Here, a small fleet of temporal monitoring stations circles lazily above the fertile landscapes of Old Earth, circa 1979.*

LEFT
The Starcutter *This was the United Federation World's most notable post-Interregnum passenger liner. Built at a time when Interworlds Thruspace Co. had captured the bulk of the passenger and mail service between the colony worlds, her design had to fulfil the twin requirements of the 17 day 'thru space' interstellar service, and the more relaxed, visually more accommodating long range Einvelocity cruise. Overall length 2,500 feet; mass 230,000 tons; space displacement 48 ziemen; C-holding factor 26.8–33.3; maximum Einvelocity $C \times 8$, with five second/minute time displacement.*

BELOW
TG Pieria *The Trans Galactic Company's range of smaller custom-built cruisers and private thru space luxury yachts is well illustrated by the Pieria. On the larger size, she was an Ames-driven vessel with a thru space displacement of only five ziemen, although her mass at 10,000 tons was well into the Lamming band of the quark-shift scale (28 eans). She could accommodate 50 passengers in 40 cabins, and like all TG Co. ships was equipped with Wingrove rapid-fatigue weapons systems.*

from *The Mote in God's Eye*, has made a journey from the Coal Sack Nebula by light sail, and is now travelling at six percent of the speed of light; the problem is that whereas light *pressure* can be 'tacked against' to turn the ship or slow it down, the stellar wind in the true void, which is all atomic nuclei, imparts velocity by striking and sticking to the sail and the sail cannot be moved to slow the arriving probe. It's on collision course with the Sun.

Space ship propulsion has always been carefully considered in sf, and effort is often made unnecessarily to try and describe just *how* a ship is exceeding the speed of light. Larry Niven is credited with first using the ramjet or ramscoop, a giant mouth on the front of the space vessel sucking up interstellar hydrogen and blasting it out the back. Ion drives and photon drives abounded in the fiction at a time when such ways of motive power were still theoretical and exciting. The chemical drive has rarely been used to do otherwise than launch the fictional space machine into orbit, and thence to the void.

Perhaps the most unusual star drive in fiction is Robert Sheckley's Pusher, from his story 'Specialist'. The Ship of this story is made up of alien beings, each with a different function, Walls, Feeder, Doctor, Talker etc. After a photon storm the Pusher is killed, the drive therefore out of service. Human beings, it seems, are immature Pushers, and one is swiftly recruited to help. To defy Einstein, and to travel across the void in a few minutes or hours at faster than light speed needs every ounce of bluster and fictional talent if the hard-core reader is to be convinced that such a feat is possible. The *USS Enterprise*, famous ship of *Star Trek*, travels in warp space, the warp factor being the number of times faster than light she travels. Jump space is much the same thing. In Isaac Asimov's novels the jump through hyperspace is accompanied by a stomach-wrenching nausea, but jump space is virtually instantaneous travel. More often hyperspace is a weird and wonderful universe, where nothing is real and the stars stream like liquid. Remember the Star Gate sequence from

2001: A Space Odyssey? Visually tremendous, but fiction can evoke a similar sense of wonder as the Star Gate is passed, and the strange, dimensionless area of hyper/under/sub/thru/space is dramatically traversed.

Mind you, things can sometimes go wrong even with such sophisticated devices as the hyperjumpdrive. In Poul Anderson's now classic *Tau Zero*, a space ship cannot stop its steady acceleration towards the ultimate upper limit of velocity, the speed of light, but because of relativity, everything is distorted as Tau Zero is reached, that final moment before the ultimate speed of light; the ship is gigantic, time is meaningless, and every shudder and tremble in the hull of the vessel is just another universe being knocked aside as the ship streaks onwards.

Space ships have taken a multitude of forms during the short history of the fantastic, from the bullets of the Victorians, to the dart-shaped craft of classic pre-war pulps, from the enormous many-portholed battle cruisers of E. E. 'Doc' Smith, to the weird, cylindrical Heechee craft of Fred Pohl's *Gateway*, from the coffin that takes C. S. Lewis' hero to Perelandra (Venus), to the complex and enormous space ship of Kubrick's *2001*.

Those bullet-shaped space craft appear over and over again in the early days, their occupants clinging desperately to slings or hammocks to cushion themselves against the shock of being blasted into space from the muzzle of some gigantic gun. Wells had his Martians invade the earth in this way,

The IC Ortygia *A typical cargo-liner, she was built in circum Vega orbit for the Interstar Carriage Company of the Small Federated Worlds, a long established thru space cargo firm set up in the early days of the Second Federation. Their major routes include the Procyon to Ree'hdworld, and Aldeberan IV to Holman's World routes, both of which are now dangerous war zones. The Ortygia was launched on Jubilee Day 4578 AD, and to demonstrate her cargo-carrying capacity took an initial cargo of 12,000 Mc units of irenium to the Research World complex of Bianco's Star in what was to have been just over 27 days real-time. Her time displacement was ten seconds/minute, causing critical mass to be reached in 15 days, with a quark duplication factor of 85 percent. The ship exploded, giving rise to the so-called Octopus Nebula.*

RIGHT
The UF Way Station *The Way Station's owners, Rim Liners Galactic Ltd, a small subsidiary company of the Federation, judged that as a single unit she could not be operated profitably on the regular circumgalactic routes through the dustfree gulfs between the spiral arms, and so she was adapted for luxury service running between Old Earth and the Abreides Star Cluster, reputedly the richest group of worlds (47) in the Galaxy. Her old-fashioned design made her something of a novelty—she was modelled on 22nd century interplanetary Solar cruisers and cargo carriers—but also meant she was subject to gravitic stress.*

BELOW
Cable & Thru Space Co. *During the early years of the First Federation, Cable and Wireless expanded to become the Cable and Thru Space Co. and gained a virtual monopoly on intergalactic communication systems. Shown here are examples of their relay station servicing 'crusoid', a 250 yard long, 400,000 ton Ames-driven vessel capable of serving and maintaining 45,000 thru space relay satellites.*

and Verne visited the Moon; Korda's magnificent film of *Shape of Things to Come* shot two young astronaut heroes to the stars from a gun whose recoil, at blast-off, killed thousands. Gravity in the early part of this century was abused quite as much as Einsteinian physics is abused today, for the sake of a good story, for the sake of literature blissfully unencumbered by such trivia as the mechanics of the universe.

The rocket ship was an American fictional invention, certainly deriving from European research. The space ships of early pulp literature are all slender, streamlined, point-nosed craft, standing somewhere in the desert, on four wide fins. Look at *Tin Tin*, the great Belgian comic-strip, to see the stereotype wonderfully satirised in his adventures on the Moon. The ships were built in the middle of nowhere, and occasionally in a back yard, and they lurched to the heavens on great spumes of flame, and onwards through infinity on great spumes of flame, and thence down to Mars . . . on great spumes of

flame: but it was wonderful stuff, the stuff of dreams and idylls. In all his stories, Bradbury's Earthmen zip around the solar system in such tin cans, touching down here and there, their occupants leaping into the airy, breathable atmospheres of different worlds crying 'We're here!'. The stream-lining effect took ages to shake off, longer even than the realisation that ships could be built elsewhere than in the desert, or a back yard . . . they could be built in space, and they could be built any shape you liked. But to imagine such complexity required the consideration of shuttles to take the adventurers down to the planet surface. The complexity of real-life moonflight would have seemed ludicrous to the ancient science fictioneers. After all, Eric France Russell had his quarter-mile long space ship in 'And Then There Were None' bellyflop onto an alien world, gouging a mile long furrow through the earth and skidding to a stop inches away from a totally indifferent farmer. They don't make shock absorbers like they did in the 1950s. But, paradoxically, as soon as the functional fascination of the space ship had worn off, it started to be taken quite seriously as both gadget and symbol in its own right. Streamlining went by the board, a fact powerfully reinforced when Kubrick made *2001* and that long and cumbersome and totally fabulous piece of space machinery slid onto the screen from off stage left. The ship that takes Fred Pohl's young astronauts across the cosmos in 'The Gold At Starbow's End' is so tampered with, and added to as its occupants store things and build things outside it, that it ends up looking like a flying junk heap. And with the better comprehension of the needs and otherwise of space came an understanding of the cruelty of space and the fact that mass and fuel and acceleration were critically linked. Tom Godwin's story 'The Cold Equations' sets a one-man ship towards a colony world where plague has struck; the ship is carrying a payload of medical supplies so precisely computed that the total weight of cargo, ship and crew will enable it to reach the world in time to break the plague. A stowaway, a young girl hoping to see her brother on the same planet, adds so much extra mass that the ship will not make it in time. The cold equation, and the only solution, is to jettison her. Robert Heinlein had played with much the same problem a

few years before in 'Skylift', exploring the problem of the G-force involved in accelerating to speeds sufficient to set a ship across the void at close to the speed of light. When a plague breaks out on Proserpina Station, on far off Pluto, a 'torch' (astronaut) must be found whose body can take three and a half G acceleration for over nine days so that supplies can be got through.

A space ship is more than the man who rides it, however, and sf was quick to realise the fact. Anne McCaffrey's Helva from 'The Ship Who Sang' is a perfect example of the sentient space ship, the machine-human complex that can function with its pilot as a unified whole. Helva has been born deformed, a 'thing' that will be condemned unless it passes the mental tests that all newborn babies have to pass. She succeeds but because of the physical deformity she is linked integrally with the metal shell of a ship:

Instead of kicking feet, Helva's neural responses started her wheels; instead of grabbing with hands she manipulated mechanical extensions.'

As she matured, more and more

Solar Federation Amusement Ship James Kirk The James Kirk, *and its sister ship the* Solar Trekkie, *were developed in the late 25th Century as part of the Orbital Festival Complex around Mars (seen in the background). Called the Las Vegas of space, the Festival Complex went bankrupt and was dismantled after some 200 years service. The two bizarre shaped, charm-powered craft (modelled after an Old Earth vidshow) were put into commercial service as hospital ships, ferrying miners from the asteroids to hospital bases on Luna and Earth itself.*

An interesting, and rather baffling postscript to the Solar Trekkie *is that in 2678 AD she was 'stolen' from Earth dock by a brigade of teenagers calling themselves the Friends of Spock. Their 14-day space jaunt was terminated when, in an effort to outrun a Federation police cruiser, they impacted with the asteroid Hermes, destroying both themselves and the asteroid, which at that time housed Brosnan Base, an Australian penal colony.*

neural synapses would be adjusted to operate other mechanisms that went into the maintenance and running of the space ship.

Helva, in fact, is the brain half of a scout ship, now called a brain ship. It's advantage is its speed of response and the fact that it cannot run rogue. Pituitary interference will keep Helva forever a midget, tightly bound to the web of the ship, operating in tandem with the pilot.

Fred Saberhagen's Berserkers are something totally different in both design and desire. They are alien, and they are robotic, intelligent ships that have been programmed to destroy practically anything and everything that looks in the least threatening to their masters, or to their masters wishes, which loosely interpreted might be: I don't like the universe, kill it! From 'Fortress World', the first of the galaxy-smashing series: 'One such machine could hang over a planet colonised by men and in two days pound the surface into a lifeless cloud of dust and steam a hundred miles deep.'

Renegade space ships abound in sf, mostly battle cruisers with robotic brains, programmed in destruction and later deserted by crew, perhaps because of plague, or because the faster

than light drive failed several thousand years ago. They come out of the void upon unsuspecting colony worlds and they can only be argued out of their programme of destruction by the most impeccable logic. Norman Spinrad's episode of *Star Trek*, 'The Doomsday Machine', is one of the best explorations of this theme.

Giant space ships are not always the order of the day. In Katherine Maclean's exquisite story 'Pictures Don't Lie' a ship full of humanoid aliens is making its first contact with Earth, and over the view-screen the alien visitors can be seen to be moving in peculiarly slow motion, but no one is too worried about that. The ship lands in a nearby field, but no watching Earthman can see it. When they go out to look for it one of them treads on something small and tinny: TV pictures give no impression of relative size. An alien vessel at the other end of the scale is Rama, a classic in its own time, and a truly enigmatic machine in a truly enigmatic novel by Arthur Clarke, *Rendezvous with Rama*. Simply stated, Rama is an alien space ship of vast proportion. The Earthmen who explore it can scarcely cope with its size. There are mountains and lakes fashioned upon its inner surface, and the journey through Rama takes weeks. It has swung out of interstellar space, and is passing through the solar system on its way to some unknown destination. There is intelligent life on board, but it is so huge, this ship, that none ever comes to light; perhaps the aliens are in suspended animation or perhaps they are hiding. Rama brings its message of intelligence in the universe and takes the questions and their answers away with it into the void again.

Perhaps one of the most bizarre space ships described in the fiction is Joan Vinge's 'Crystal Ship', a gigantic interstellar vessel made totally of transparent crystal; now in orbit above the Earth, its alien occupants watch the blue world below their feet as they live an idyllic inactive life, dreaming of their pasts. The scout ship *Dark Star*, from Dan O'Bannon and John Carpenter's hilarious film and book of the same name, speaks to its paranoid human crew with a lilting, sexy female voice; as they tour the Magellenic Clouds looking for things to blow up, one of the ship's bombs gets an acute case of self-awareness, not to mention irritation at being told to defuse after once being set to go. It takes things into its own fuse-wires and has to be argued out of

blowing up by the use of Cartesian logic. Unfortunately . . .

But at least the *Dark Star* has solid walls, unlike David Gerrold's *Space Skimmer*. The skimmer is a 'stasis-field' ship. It doesn't need metal walls because a field of invisible force acts as both the hull and the drive. All that can be seen are metal plates on which men stand, on either side, at any angle, each man carrying his own up-down orientation with him. In Gerrold's own words:

Starflake! That was his first impression. Something bright and gold and glimmering, flashing shades of yellow and red and flickering white . . . dazzling vanes of silver and emerald, amethyst and opal, moonstone and ruby and diamond—some sculptural, clustered, reaching, describing and fulfilling the shape of a spherical sunburst—

An original ship indeed, and so different from the United States Star ship *Roger Burlingame* from Gerrold's appalling novel *Yesterday's Children*. The *Burlingame* looks, feels, performs and is staffed precisely like the *USS Enterprise*. A manic crew of cardboard characters race the *Burlingame* from one end of the galaxy to the other, pursuing what is affectionately known as a 'bogie', an alien vessel in desperate need of blowing up. The 'bogie' turns out to be their own reflection in the universe, and not before time the *Burlingame* mercifully vanishes up its own exhaust jets.

Passenger ships and cruisers take humanity across the void; scout ships and space skimmers seek out strange new worlds; battle cruisers and battle tugs police the void, their phaser banks and blasters primed and trembling with orgasmic pressure; but the cities in space wander aimlessly, deriving all that they need to function from the empty reaches. James Blish's Okies are perhaps classics of their kind, entire cities enclosed in transparent domes, lifted from their original ground on Earth at the end of huge anti-gravity engines called Spindizzies. They have become the traders of the stars, and known now as Okies, the cities of Scranton, New York, Pittsburgh and others, all the great industrial cities, have lifted themselves away from the face of the Earth; equipped with the new

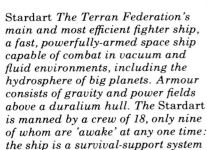

Stardart *The Terran Federation's main and most efficient fighter ship, a fast, powerfully-armed space ship capable of combat in vacuum and fluid environments, including the hydrosphere of big planets. Armour consists of gravity and power fields above a duralium hull. The Stardart is manned by a crew of 18, only nine of whom are 'awake' at any one time: the ship is a survival-support system with organic synthesiser units and suspended animation capability. Powered by Ames drive, alternating with conventional light-pressure booster jets, the Dart's main weapons innovation is CLAWS, the Complete Log Axis Weapons System, a laser device running the entire length of the ship. It is also equipped with pin mines, projectiles, blaster banks and Wingrove Weapons Systems.*

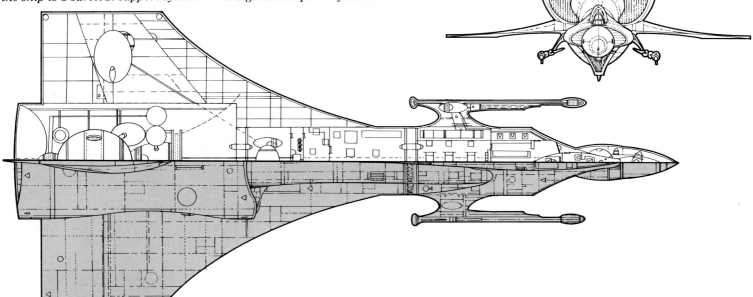

longevity drugs they are making a life for the stars.

But the Okie cities are not alone in the void. Far from Earth, the Interstellar Space society known as Retort City, floats as if transfixed in the blackness of space, midway between Altair and Barnard's Star. Barrington Bayley's splendid novel *Collision Course* describes how Retort City is a city in a bottle, its outer skin being transparent and glassy so that an observer watching from space might discern within the glass envelope a sort of double spindle, the general plan of the city's internal structure, a muted blaze of lights and moving shapes. The weird fact about Retort City as that time is moving in different directions in either end of the bottle.

Cities of a different sort are the generation ships, and science fiction was quick to realise that, without the secret of faster than light travel, a ship capable of supporting several hundred generations of potential planetary colonists would be the only way to conquer the stars. It doesn't always work out too well. The ship that plods the void in A. E. van Vogt's 'Far Centaurus' takes hundreds of years to reach Alpha Centauri, one of its crew awakening every 50 years from suspended animation to check that all systems are still go. When it reaches the star it finds, of course, that technology has raced ahead back on Earth and the galaxy has been long conquered by light-drives. But what happens inside the ships is often fun, because inevitably the original purpose is lost, and the gigantic generation vessel becomes the entire universe to those who live inside the steel shell. The arrogant young boy in J. G. Ballard's 'Thirteen To Centaurus' spots a hole in the ship's hull and finds himself peering out into the great warehouse where the 'Generation Ship Experiment' is being housed, but things are not so pat in Brian Aldiss's *Nonstop* where the hydroponics have got out of control and the entire ship is a jungle. Clifford Simak's 'Target Generation' shows how religious belief might arise from ancient memories of Earth, as God is no longer worshipped,

Archie Bunker goes to the Stars
A scene from the immensely popular 24th century vidshow of this name. Archie Bunker, mortally offended at having to accept refuelling from a red-painted relay station run by Jewish-Vegan cross breeds, has shot a blaster hole through the hull of his space cruiser the Middle America. *He now attempts to repair the damage while his daughter holds his snaking cable and uses her thru space transmitter to try and convince him that cutting the metal skin from the now redundant heat shields at the front of the cruiser can in no way achieve this.*

Interstellar Refuelling Station *In the days before thru space, a large chemical fuel consignment was important on every vessel travelling in Einvelocity in order to 'nudge' the ship, since gravity-well and Black Star influences effectively pulled the ship off course. When the requirement for chemical fuel ceased, the relay stations were adapted as interstellar restaurants and relaxation centres. Named after Old English motorway stations, this particular stopover, in the Orion sector, was called New Port Paganal.*

and instead it is the Great Tree that is the focus of spiritual life; the ship probes onwards, outwards, generation after generation, and inevitably a youngster and his mate break out of the rules of ship society, explore the forbidden passages—in the ship, that is—and find themselves on different deck levels; ultimately they reach the control room where the ship's programme is logged, allowing them to work things out. Harry Harrison's hollow asteroid with its Aztec culture on the surface and ultra-technological culture in the tunnels below, bridges the gap between the concept of cities in flight and that of the generation ship.

The trouble with generation ships is that they make obeisance to relativity as she is known and understood. No such restrictions for the inimitable E. E. 'Doc' Smith, whose Lensmen are among the most classic of all the galaxy-blasting, ultra right-wing super space heroes. Not for Smith the subtle description of space ship details; his super dreadnoughts are either spherical or cigar-shaped and covered with portholes, but one thing is for sure . . . they are truly BIG, and we are told over and

over again that the size of them defies the human mind to grasp the full dimensions. His description of a space port and the super dreadnought *Chicago* from First Lensman:

Samms could scarcely keep from flinching, That featureless, grey, smoothly curving wall of alloy steel loomed so incredibly high above them—extended so terrifyingly far outwards beyond its visible means of support! It *must* be on the verge of crashing!

But it isn't of course, and as is pointed out to the intrepid Samms, 'scaring hell out of them on the ground has one big advantage; they felt so safe inside that they didn't get the collywobbles so bad when they went free'. No space collywobbles, perhaps, but a certain stomach-wrenching nausea one hopes as the giant super dreadnought space cruisers lurch upwards to the void:

Through the lower, denser layers of atmosphere the *Chicago* bored in seconds; then, as the air grew thinner, she rushed upwards faster and faster. Being completely without inertia the ship's velocity was at every instant that at which the friction of the

23

LEFT
The Great Explosion *The massive expansion outwards to the stars, so often predicted in the primitive fictions of the 19th and 20th centuries, began to occur in the latter years of the 25th century, when the critical relationship between time displacement and quark energy was discovered. In this painting by the contemporary artist Patrick Woodroffe, some of the earlier interstellar vessels are shown, cumbersome, ugly craft, laden down with chemical fuel and unnecessary supplies. The success rate of the early interstellar voyages was less than 25 percent.*

BELOW
Cities in Flight *During the early part of the First Empire, a number of overcrowded cities from the American mainland were isolated from the Earth's crust and projected into space on unwieldy but efficient anti-gravity devices called Spindizzies. The AG devices were never used commercially for space shipping. Here the city of Scranton can be seen awaiting a supplies exchange visit from a small, interplanetary trading vessel.*

medium through which she blasted her way equalled precisely the force of her driving thrust.

And there is no arguing with a drive mechanism like *that*!

When all said and done, the fictional use of space ships has been predominantly as functional units of hardware, not requiring much description beyond a cursory reference to gaping ramjets, or a smooth alloy steel hull; where a ship is more than just a transport convenience, it has been invaluable as a symbol of course, a solid steel and glass metaphor for all manner of things. And quite naturally, because of its customary along, cylindrical shape, and habit of penetrating, even *thrusting*, out into the womb-like void of the universe, the space ship has acquired a reputation as a different type of symbol. If cars are considered to be phallic symbols, it isn't surprising to find a similar psychological indulgence being taught about the rocket ship; but really it's only in the art that any unconscious or conscious awareness of the sexual nature of the star ship is demonstrated. Fiction

Canyon Launch *The Panglobal
Ocean and Deep Space
Administration (PODSA!) were
responsible for building 20
duel-function research and launch
platforms during the earliest days of
interplanetary exploration. The Dorey
platforms—after the designer—
could float on oceans or in air gaps
in canyons and launch themselves on
chemical fuel into orbital space, and
thence move onwards between planets.
Part of their success was the use of
several small AG M-repulsion drives,
thought to be precursors of the bigger,
more powerful Spindizzy. Most of the
Dorey platforms are now in circum
Saturn orbit.*

Irrikon Space City *This enormous
interstellar City was one of a fleet of
such city/battle stars that arrived
from intergalactic space, possibly from
the M31 galaxy, and went into deep
orbit about the double star system of
Cassiopeia. Little contact was
established with the inhabitants—
small humanoids, with insectoidal
features and large, membranous
wings—but a few unwary Federation
vessels were discouraged from coming
too close by having non-vital hull
sections shot at. The Irrikon vessels
remained in Federation space during
most of the Second Empire, before
moving out of the galaxy and out of
contact. It is estimated that each city
housed more than two million
inhabitants. The likeliest explanation
for their state of travel and existence
is that their home star went nova and
the entire Irrikonian population was
forced to take up a nomadic life.*

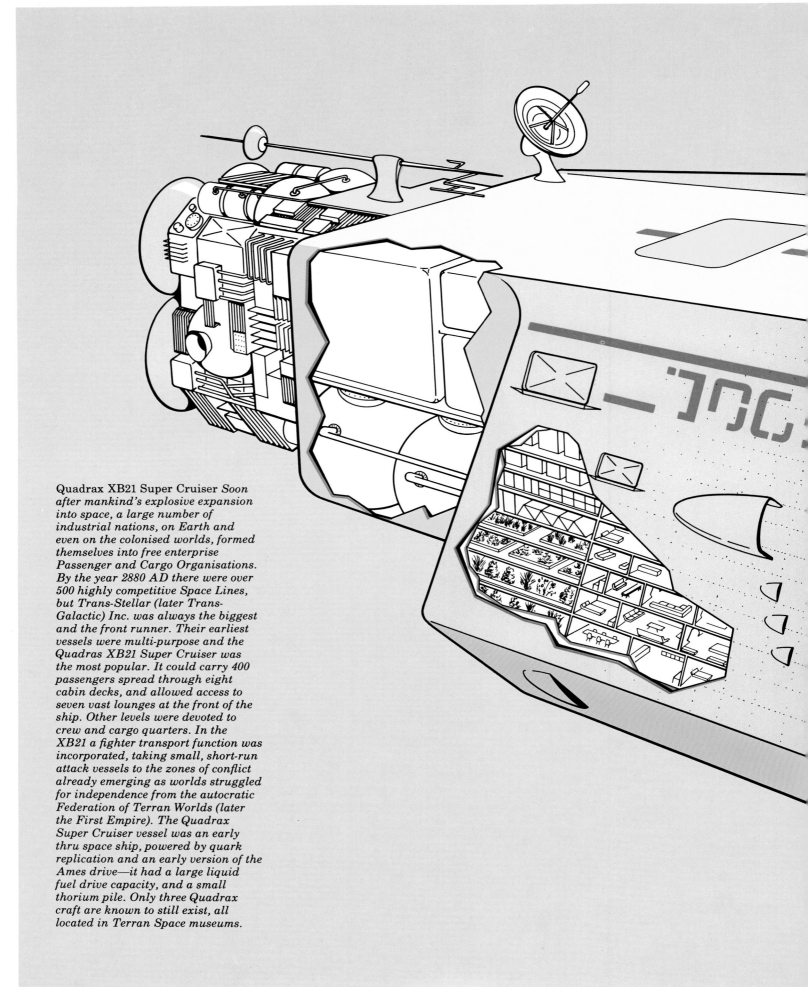

Quadrax XB21 Super Cruiser *Soon after mankind's explosive expansion into space, a large number of industrial nations, on Earth and even on the colonised worlds, formed themselves into free enterprise Passenger and Cargo Organisations. By the year 2880 AD there were over 500 highly competitive Space Lines, but Trans-Stellar (later Trans-Galactic) Inc. was always the biggest and the front runner. Their earliest vessels were multi-purpose and the Quadras XB21 Super Cruiser was the most popular. It could carry 400 passengers spread through eight cabin decks, and allowed access to seven vast lounges at the front of the ship. Other levels were devoted to crew and cargo quarters. In the XB21 a fighter transport function was incorporated, taking small, short-run attack vessels to the zones of conflict already emerging as worlds struggled for independence from the autocratic Federation of Terran Worlds (later the First Empire). The Quadrax Super Cruiser vessel was an early thru space ship, powered by quark replication and an early version of the Ames drive—it had a large liquid fuel drive capacity, and a small thorium pile. Only three Quadrax craft are known to still exist, all located in Terran Space museums.*

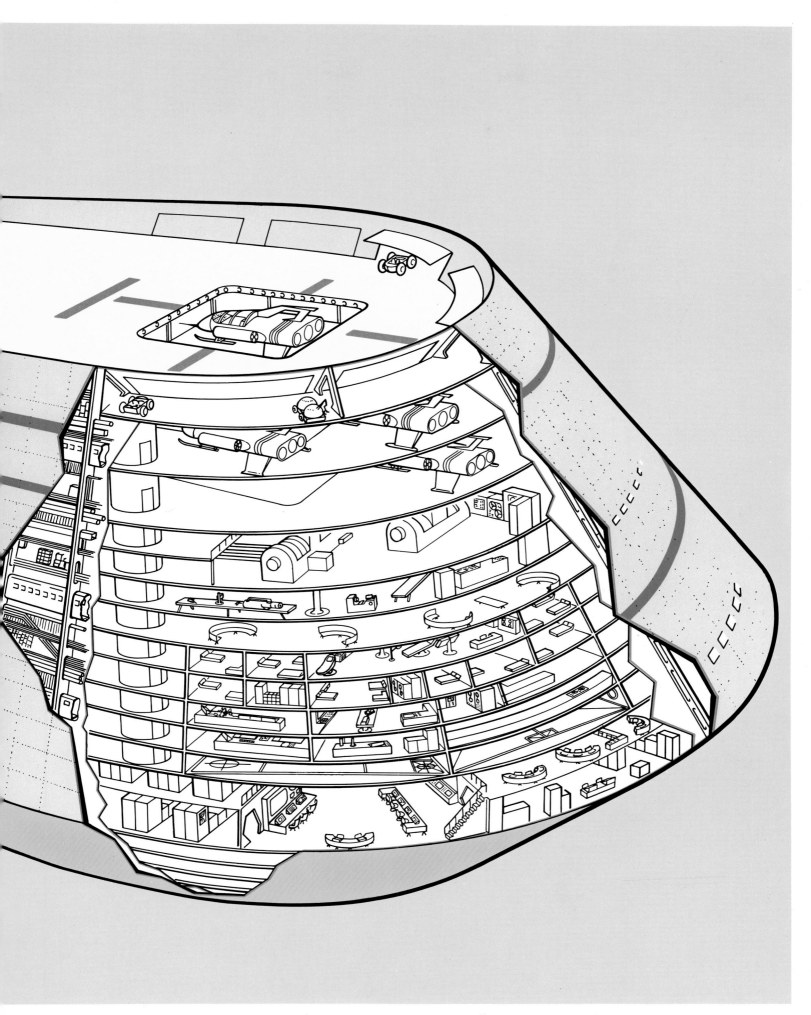

LEFT
Inter System Public Transport Cruiser, the Byron Lizzard
nicknamed the 'spider', the ISPT passenger cruiser Byron Lizzard went into service some time in the early 29th century, when interstellar flight was still in its infancy. The passenger cruiser line was designed to make cheap circum solar system flight was still in its infancy. The astronomical and drive research, though these functions were never really adopted. The great problem with the Lizzard was its cumbersome grip on space and its terrible high atmosphere characteristics: when in close planetary orbit it required an 'elevator tug', shown here, to maintain its orbit. It was scrapped after a few years and replaced by the more efficient and more popular Sidey 'Pulse' Cruiser series which combined streamlining with deep space manoeuvring characteristics unusual in a nonmilitary solar craft. ISPT eventually became the Trans Galactic Company and not Inter Worlds Thruspace as is commonly believed.

LEFT
The UF Isaac Asimov *The Isaac Asimov's service was a circum galactic route between Trantor and Proxyon III, at that time a major industrial world. She was designed during the transitional period between the First and Second Federations, a timespan (Earth relative) of 60 years. This was a time when free enterprise and invention were unbounded, and a number of unusual designs were emerging from the industrial worlds, vessels that could double in function as passenger and industrial freighters. Length 36,000 feet; mass 280,000 tons; space displacement 56 ziemen; C-holding factor 28.4 (29.1 unloaded); matter regeneration capability unusually high at 12 hf and she was equipped with two 14hf stion producing Amesdrives; maximum Einvelocity C × 4, with a three second/minute time displacement at highest velocity.*

The Rohan-Langford 'Deaf Ear'
Subspace Jamming System *This is an
early version, shown operating close
to the Zone Wars battle region in the
Hounslow Nebula.*

may deal with ships, like giant sperms,
flooding outwards to seed egg-shaped
worlds with the new human life, but it's
the cover artist who juxtaposes the
space ship and the beautiful, usually
skimpily clad woman.

It's hard, though, to look at a Chris
Foss space ship and see a symbol of anything. Jagged, deformed, weird, sus-
piciously reminiscent of items of
household furniture, they stand apart
in sf art as probably being far more
practically realistic than any streamlined stellar cruiser, too big to cope
with gravity, and yet still fashioned
with aerodynamic precision, presum-
ably ready to cope with those gusty solar
winds. Foss has made an artform of the
hideous; he has painted a sense of
wonder from the epileptic combination
of bits and panels and frames and pipes.
It is really difficult to choose between
his totally individual vision of the
fantastic future of hardware and, say,

Chris Moore's precision paintings of
Pan Am space craft approaching the
towering, stratospheric navigation
buildings of his future space port.

Space debris *An impression of the
pre-Terran debris found orbiting the
beautiful world SeemonStar, and
believed to have originated from an
Empire founded in the Sagittarian
Galactic Zone by precursors of the
present day Ja'cracharakk. These
peaceful, rather primitive aliens
inhabit three worlds in the same star
system, indicating their original
ability to travel in space.*

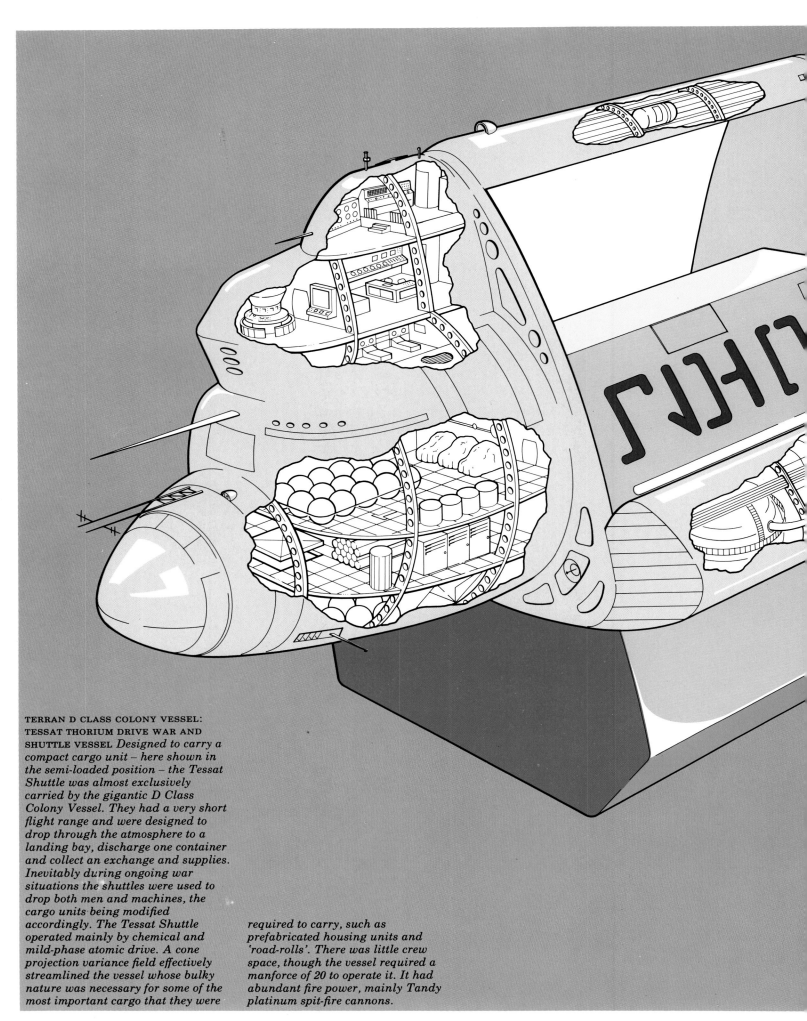

**TERRAN D CLASS COLONY VESSEL:
TESSAT THORIUM DRIVE WAR AND
SHUTTLE VESSEL** *Designed to carry a
compact cargo unit – here shown in
the semi-loaded position – the Tessat
Shuttle was almost exclusively
carried by the gigantic D Class
Colony Vessel. They had a very short
flight range and were designed to
drop through the atmosphere to a
landing bay, discharge one container
and collect an exchange and supplies.
Inevitably during ongoing war
situations the shuttles were used to
drop both men and machines, the
cargo units being modified
accordingly. The Tessat Shuttle
operated mainly by chemical and
mild-phase atomic drive. A cone
projection variance field effectively
streamlined the vessel whose bulky
nature was necessary for some of the
most important cargo that they were
required to carry, such as
prefabricated housing units and
'road-rolls'. There was little crew
space, though the vessel required a
manforce of 20 to operate it. It had
abundant fire power, mainly Tandy
platinum spit-fire cannons.*

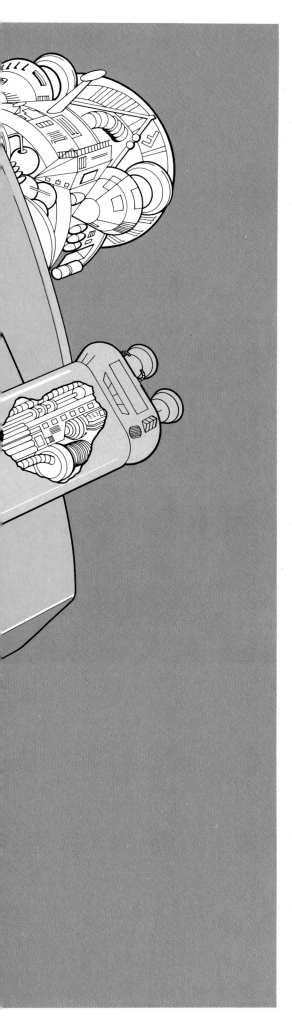

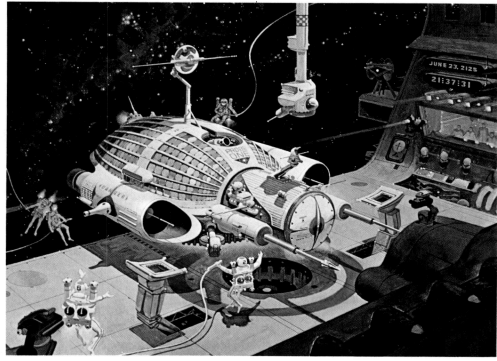

ABOVE
Terran D Class Colony Vessel:
Scout and Recognisance Ship *Four
man, sub-light vessels designed to
orbit in high and low trajectories
around any target planet for three to
four weeks. Each colony ship carried
20 such scout ships, which on
landing could be modified into land,
sea or air craft.*

BELOW
Terran D Class Colony Vessel:
Command Centre *This extensible
command centre could be withdrawn
behind 30 foot thick duralium shields.
The colony vessels were passenger/
war ships combined, but because so
much of their bulk was taken up with
the provisions and cargo for the New
World, they usually routed around
war zones, travelling at very low C
velocities.*

Interplanetary Wars and Weapons

'... the value of human life is zero the machines become the heroes'

War may be·hell, but to the science fiction writer war is paradise, ready-made drama, endlessly variable as he explores Star Wars, or Insect Wars, or Mind Wars, or even Witch Wars. With the great explosion outwards to the stars, and the explosion of population that goes with it, the value of human life is seen to diminish almost to zero; the machines of war become the heroes, and war itself becomes a symbol of man's dominance, not just of his own concrete-polluted world, but of everything in the universe. The warships get bigger, the weapons more horrific, the ways of death more variable.

War in scientific romance began early; H. G. Wells described the hideous events and aftermath of a Martian invasion of the Earth. *The War of the Worlds* was a war of territory. Mars, overcrowded and exhausted, sends its warships—or war bullets—to Earth's green pastures, where there is room to live and breathe again.

Thereafter Earth was invaded more times than most readers care to remember. They have come from all across the universe to take our land, or inhabit our

'Dustbowl' *This was the name given to Attack Station KGx/46, one of the largest of the interplanetary combat stations and war refuges ever launched by the Terran military during the 70 years of the Zone Wars. Its name came from its regular tour of duty through the Coal Sack Nebula, and its specially fitted ramscoops, designed to suck up interstellar matter and accelerate it to high velocity. Special features of all such stations were Rohan-Langford 'Deaf Ear' underspace jamming systems, Elerac KTH new weapons couplings, and K.Y.L.E. brain-scramblers for use against military robots. Its fire power was immense, with over 40,000 multi-vac controlled laser systems. It could transport a military crew of 20,000, plus equipment and supplies for ten years. It was defended by ultra-screens, but its 40 foot thick titanium steel hull served better against such torpedo or blaster attacks, as is shown here.*

seas, or exploit and subdue our peoples. Some of them have come, as in Eric Frank Russell's 'Into Your Tent I'll Creep', and discovered that the true intelligence on Earth is not man at all, but the dog. Others have come not in war, but in peace, but the generals have always overruled the voices of reason with their paranoid hearts of steel, and the tanks fire on defenceless flying saucers, or the revolting alien forms are cut down in machine gun swathes before they can utter some memorable epithet upon their arrival.

They don't all come in peace, of course, and the atmosphere of Earth has often been rent by the screech of the invasion fleets. Sometimes the invaders are hideous slug-like creatures, as in Robert Heinlein's *The Puppet Masters*, which attach themselves to the spines of human beings and take them over; sometimes they take over the minds of human beings, destroying all trace of awareness and using the corpses like machines—for example, *The Invasion of the Body Snatchers*. Sometimes the green-skinned, humanoid, muscle-bound invaders stalk the land, physically subduing the peoples, but falling prey to the ways and wiles, tricks and psychological manipulations of our most resistant and superior species. Eric Frank Russell, Robert Silverberg and Christopher Anvil had immense fun with this theme in the 1950s, showing the many ways that man can outthink, outsmart, and cunningly trick the alien invader, despite his immense technological superiority. I don't care how intelligent you make an alien, declared John Campbell to his authors, just so long as man always comes out on top! And man always does come out on top, in pulp fiction and

LEFT
Arisian mercenaries *During the Final War, between the industrial planetary systems of Saros and Tucana M, a large number of Arisian and Durinian mercenaries were recruited for land-based combat. Their flexiarmour is an irenium-titanium-carboncord fabric, but their helmets are pure iron, and show the tribal horns of the Arisian. Their weapons are Federation supply, mark 6 beamers, with a fire output of 400 contact explosive pellets per second.*

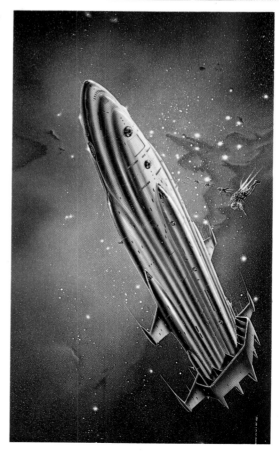

RIGHT
Starship Troopers *The jetpropelled infantrymen of the interstellar void seen here on manoeuvres about their transport cruiser, a specially fitted thru space cargo liner built originally by Interstellar Colonial Corporation and later modified and armed for use in the Zone Wars.*

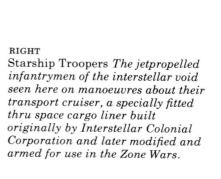

even later. In John Wyndham's classic novel *The Day of the Triffids* the alien plant-like creatures, activated when they sense that the human population had gone blind, begin their prepared programme of invasion. They kill all but a handful of human beings who finally escape to an island beyond the range of the triffid spores. Man loses. But the film industry, bristling at the implication that man and triffid might be at least equals, find sea water is the way to kill the film's mindless plants. H. G. Wells' set the precedent for a *deus ex machina* ending when his Martians died of terrestrial bacterial infection; it was a neat twist and a logical one, because the Martians came unprepared; today it is far more likely that an invasion from space would result in our losing. It's hard to swallow, but it makes more sense. Even E. E. 'Doc' Smith realised that any race capable of crossing the void would be possessed of potent and sinister weaponry, and would swiftly reduce man's cities, and man himself, to a molten rubble; from *Triplanetary*, as the invading ship sucks the metal from our world:

> The Nevian vessel hung poised in full visibility high above the metropolis. Scornful of the pitiful weapons wielded by man, she hung there, her sinister beauty of line sharply defined against the cloudless sky. From her shining hull there reached down a tenuous but rigid rod of crimson energy . . . Office buildings, skyscrapers towering majestically in their architectural symmetry, collapsed into heaps of debris as their steel skeletons were abstracted.

Man also wars against man, of course, and often this is for territory and often for something called an ideological clash. Inevitably his transglobal skirmishes end in a radiation wasteland, the holocaust reducing the world to rubble. Survivors, resistance members, returning spacemen, all crawl through this rubble and eventually rebuild civilisation, society and, of course, weapons.

LEFT
The Earthship (ES) Lifebane *Seen after her dramatic crash in the tropics of Old Earth, the* Lifebane *had for many years been considered unsuitable for war service. Her 'space injection' drive (visible now that desert nomads have stripped away much of the lead-tungsten shielding) could not propel her at more than twice the speed of light, and her time displacement was huge, thus restricting her to very short trips. Her armaments were primitive —mostly blasters, macro-beams and Parker mark 5 blister skins. She was shot down over Earth by a Faberian Soudot Class cruiser.*

RIGHT
The Dorey-Montgomery Metal CPs *These were robots fully adapted to land-based war and equipment carriage. Used during the early years of the Zone Wars, they proved ineffective against the rapidly developed beam guns. Over 40 million CPs (complex positrons) were built. They stood nine feet tall and had phospho-iodine retinal wide-view perceptors and a programmable capacity of over 20,000 alternative instructions, all carried by a single cellular chip complex linked with the standard copper and sodium positronic brain system. Unable to kill or harm the enemy, they were effective at disarming and imprisoning them. Unfortunately, any slight damage to the cellular chip could cause aggressive tendencies to develop in their behaviour, and they could as easily turn against their own army. They were replaced with automatic weapons systems after the battle of Jackson's Rift on Algol 3.*

That particular irony was realised long ago, and perhaps has been explored best in Walter Miller's award-winning novel *A Canticle for Liebowitz*. Hundreds of novels have had man grubbing up out of the radiation dust of his own senseless power-flexing, and the post-disaster theme is almost a cliché now. Some novels stand apart, however, for having explored the war wasteland and after in truly imaginative ways:

For a really big war, though the Earth is not room enough, and man takes to the stars, where his super dreadnoughts can be constructed on an infinitely large scale. Space war, star wars, interplanetary attack, all of this has a sickening romance to it, the Battle of Britain transferred to the stars where ships explode soundlessly and human screams are lost against the silence of the void. It's all so clean, so sterile, so civilised and technologically

LEFT
LEFT
Startling War *How they saw space war and interplanetary attack in the days before man had achieved control of the air. This old picture from a science prediction magazine of the 17th or 18th century was used recently as a morale booster for troops based on the Lyran worlds and engaged in fighting the forces of the Thangan Empire. It shows fire-driven rocket ships blasting the sort of brick and steel building that was replaced during the Recession of the 23rd century by low, transparo-steel pyramids such as now cover the Earth.*

LEFT
A King Crab *This armoured pursuit and attack machine was nicknamed the King Crab because of its immense extensile arms that can reach from below the titanium alloy carapace and lift the bulky vehicle up or down sheer cliffs. It could move at a surface speed of 85 mph, was operated by two men and could sustain fire (contact adhesive/exposive button shells) for four hours. Used during the Lyran Wars, this one is being attacked by a tribesman of the colonised world of Newgrange. The tribes were ultimately decimated as the war swept across their lands.*

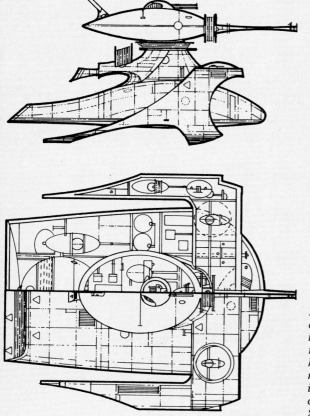

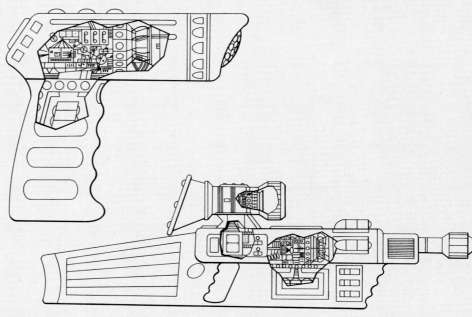

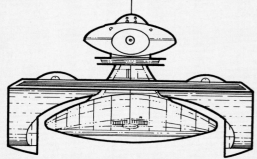

Auran Hand Weapons *Captured from dead 'marines' after a brief skirmish in the high atmosphere and sub-void reaches of Trifarian III (an important heavy planet). The hand gun is a multi-beam gamma radiation intensifier—the stock holds 20 power cylinders giving a total firing time of 20 years.*

The rifle—cumbersome to a Human— is designed to stop heavy armoured vehicles by use of pulse-exploding korium power studs, over 200 of which are stored in the stock. The sighting mechanism includes an eye-blink trigger.

Faberian Phase-Attack Craft *This tiny vessel, built early in the skirmishes with the Faberian Principality, was capable of materialising out of thru space above a Terran colony, cutting through atmospheric layers and strafing the installations below, before dropping a single Meson bomb, known as a crustbuster because of its immense destructive power. Meson bombs were banned by mutual treaty, since whole worlds were being destroyed.*

RIGHT
Auran Attack Craft *An unusual view of an attack in progress by a squadron of these tiny, ion-driven Auran high atmosphere and low space attack craft. The Auran pilot has control only of weapons systems, the craft being a 'brain' craft with a very high decision-making faculty. Full specifications are uncertain, but they are thought to be ½C craft with no thru space capacity.*

superior, so exciting: the battle fleets lined up on each side of the tiny contested world, the lancing phaser banks, the shimmering defensive screens, the disintegrator rays sweeping across the pot-bellied hull of some immense star vessel, the space torpedoes tracking down the attack vessels and causing, just briefly, an explosion of light and heat, a tiny human nova against the backdrop of the stars. There are aliens out there, and often it is best to shoot first and ask questions later; after all, many of those aliens are hideous, and insectoidal, such as the ant masters of Venus in Ralph Milne Farley's *The Radio Beasts*, against whom man makes

swift and savage war; or the rarely seen, insectoidal aliens in Heinlein's *Starship Troopers*. The gun speaks a far more eloquent message than any clumsy attempts to communicate intelligently; besides, being non-human it is quite obvious that any alien is in fact *less* than human. We've seen this before, of course, in the pioneering American West; it is the pioneering spirit that underlies all of science fiction's galactic explorations and star wars, because they are often wars of fear, not wars of conquest. Man can easily see himself as too intelligent, too advanced in the fantastic future to want to take over inhabited worlds by force, but of course the best means of defence is attack, and he is quick off the mark when it comes to striking a blow for liberty. Aliens, then, but also renegade colonies, seeded worlds that have caught up with the homeworld and now decide to take things into their own hands, as in Edmund Hamilton's *Battle for the Stars*:

In the vastness of space the two fleets hurtled towards each other at unbelievable speeds—they were not officially at war, but they *were* fighting. And the prize . . . a small planet in the back-waters of the galaxy . . . a small planet called Earth!

For the most exciting space battles, pure adventure yarns, blaster-raging

LEFT
The Wreck of the Katherine Jeury *The Federation Sting-O Class cargo freighter, the* Katherine Jeury, *was the first victim in the war against the Fanrats, the name given to the colonial worlds of the Sagittan sector, who rose against the Empire in the early days of the First Expansion. The* Kate *was carrying vats of fermentation liquor to the military base on Proxyon when she was destroyed, although the greatest explosion was from the cargo which had expanded during the heat of the beam attack.*

LEFT
Hecuban Scan-Detonating Minesweeper-Armadillo *The armadillo was a robot, wave-controlled vehicle with a top speed of 170 mph. It could be rapidly directed across the proposed landing site of a fleet or ship to clear the area of pin mines; its detonation range was one mile in radius. It went out of service when the Hecuban navy developed an orbital mine-detonation system similar to the Federation's Kane Interference Scan.*

Chain Saw Massacre *Although over 2,000 intrasystems wars are known to have been fought during the span of the Second Empire, only a handful were properly documented logistically. This bizarre 'Chain Saw', over 6,000 feet high, is thought to have been used in the conflict over irenium supplies from the planetoid Arkus, which was contested by both Earth-type worlds of the same system of New Draco.*

Triplanetary, perhaps the most famous of his epics, battle is joined for the control of the entire universe. The Arisians, benevolent humanoids who have declared themselves guardians of civilisation, make war with the Eddoreans, shapeless malevolent beings, hungry for power at any cost. They fight on both physical and mental levels, wielding weaponry of inconceivably destructiveness. Their battleground, of course, is a tiny planet in the backwaters of a remote galaxy: Earth! The swamping of Atlantis, the fall of Rome, the wars that rack the worlds and blaze through space—all may seem historical accidents to the men involved, but each in reality is a new move in a savage universe-wide power struggle. And when Earth gets involved, and the Lensmen, and they pitch their own gigantic war vessels against the common enemy, all hell breaks loose. And yet, in such magnificent battles, the ultra-screens seem to stand up to it all, and even the fabric of space cracks and crumbles at the onslaught of such power before the alien's Nevian screens give way. To break the deadlock, then, the Ultimate Weapon must be used:

The macro-beams! Prodigious streamers of bluish green flame which tore savagely through course after course of Nevian screen! Malevolent fangs, driven with such power and velocity that they were

epics of the spacelanes, one must turn to E. E. 'Doc' Smith, or A. E. van Vogt. Their mighty battle dreadnoughts attack and demolish anything from space tugs to planetoids, and Chris Foss and others have captured the flavour of the raw power of these battles in many of their book cover paintings. Pulp magazine covers too are saturated with heat energy as the great ships gun downwards onto the unsuspecting worlds or enemy vessels. In Smith's

Proxyon Military Base *An interworlds 'hopper' (message carrying and official transport function) is seen approaching the Hard-Eye identification station on the asteroid known affectionately as Loon IV. The Proxyon base was established early on during the First Empire, although the use of the planet's seven moons ceased during the Interregnum.*

biting into the very walls of the enemy vessel before the amphibians knew that their defensive shells of force had been punctured.

Space adventure, in the days of the pulp magazines, led to a form of warfare, spectacular in design, colourful and cheery in execution, war without values, written in a form and for a purpose without values, exploring nothing but the sense of scale and wonder; it was naive war, and now seems tasteless. Space war is still with us in the fiction, but now it assumes

the symbolic role of all good fiction; the space war makes a statement, it explores values, human and moral, alien and ethical; perhaps, as in Heinlein's *Starship Troopers*, it expresses more of the author's prejudices than is good, more right-winged Power-is-Truth philosophy than the author intended. But the unquestioned master book of war is Joe Haldeman's rightly acclaimed *The Forever War*, which makes up for its literary lackings by presenting a bald and bitter statement of war's futility, and exquisitely uses

Nimian Battlecruiser *Few holographs or pictures have captured the futility and sadness of the Nimian invasion of Federation space as poignantly as this oil painting by an unknown war artist, dated to around the beginning of the Third Interregnum. The Nimian skull and the programmed weapons, still sporadically firing into the mud around the crashed space vessel, seem to reflect the short lived glory of this ostensibly useful alien race.*

44

RIGHT
The Defenders *A typical humanoid robot used on military installations (mostly land-based) in the early days of the Expansion, though probably not earlier than the 23rd century. The type became obsolete very quickly, replaced by the heavier, faster and more easily programmed Synhominoid Class meso-positron variety.*

the actual physical laws of the known universe to turn the ongoing war into a perfect metaphor for the novel's central statement.

The Forever War has been started by humans in the very early days of colonisation; at that time all colony ships were armed and the first time they met an alien vessel—a Tauran ship— they naturally blasted it. From that day on, for centuries, the war has continued, but it is not a war such as any writer has ever explored before. Each battle may last only days, but when a trooper returns home for leave he finds that centuries have passed. When he goes back to the battle zone, out among the stars, centuries have passed there too, his weapons and war ideas are outdated, and he needs total retraining; and of course, the aliens have developed far more sophisticated weapons in the meantime. Einsteinian relativity is the cause of the trouble, because fighting battles at near light speed gives a false sense of time—beyond the frame of the battle the universe is advancing far faster. Once a soldier has been out to the war zone there is nothing for him to do but stay there, ever learning to use new weapons, always waiting for the time when his own weapon is several centuries behind the enemy alien's weapon, and he is killed. And what weapons they have! As in *Starship Troopers* their space-suits are programmed and sophisticated, self-contained weapons in their own right, making many of the battle decisions themselves, and equipped with gadgets of war, and survival:

The suit is set up to save as much of your body as possible. If you lose part of an arm or a leg, one of sixteen razor-sharp irises closes around your limb with the force of a hydraulic press, snipping it off neatly and sealing the suit before you can die of explosive decompression. Then 'trauma maintenance' cauterizes the stump, replaces lost blood, and fills you with happyjuice and No-shock.

At no time in this endless war can you ever be sure of the enemy's current weapons status, whether they are slightly behind you technologically or have edged ahead, and can now out-rocket your Tachyon rocket, or neatly deflect your Bevawatt laser. The alien cruisers are attacked by human drones, tiny attack vessels that can fly at phenomenal velocities, and make use

RIGHT
The Ultimate Gunfight *During the interminable peace initiatives, and the concomitant ceasefires, a number of military bases on the farther worlds eased their boredom by modifying Federation war equipment into a series of deadly and efficient duelling machines. These AG units from an FMB Magnum heavy duty tank have been equipped with a variety of tachyon rockets and ultra-vaze minibeams. They shoot it out until one of the 'gunslingers' is destroyed.*

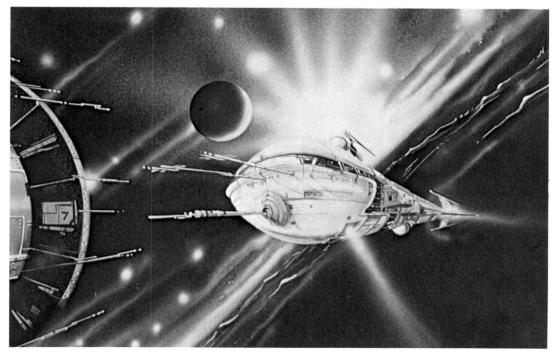

An MRTV 'DogStar' *These Military Reconnaisance Thru Space Vehicles were used to make ultra speed (approx. C × 40) journeys to enemy war zones and installation worlds, photograph, record and strafe and then return. They were called DogStars since they were first developed by Canis Weapons Inc., an industrial and armaments firm housed on Allen's World, in the Canis Major system.*

RIGHT
Arisian Assault Cruiser *The Final War, beginning as a small industrial worlds dispute, grew out of all proportion to the original squabble, as more major factions (including the Empire) used the dispute to flex their own muscles. The enormous Mother Cruiser, which could carry over a hundred 1,000-man assault cruisers in its belly, was a gift to the Sarosians from the Faberian Empire, at this time in Cold War Situation with the Human Empire.*

of any physical state in the universe, such as Black Holes or collapsars:

Instead of going into collapser insertion he had skimmed *around* the collapsar field in a slingshot orbit. He had come out going nine-tenths of the speed of light; the drones were going ·99c headed straight for the enemy cruiser. Our planet was about a thousand light-seconds from the collapsar, so the Tauran ship had only ten seconds to detect and stop both drones. At that speed it didn't matter whether you'd been hit by a nova bomb or a spitball.

The first drone, as it happens, hits the cruiser, whilst the second glides on to impact with the planet, misses by a couple of hundred kilometres and hurtles on into space, decelerating frantically: it will be back in a couple of months!

All of these memorable sf wars pale by comparison with Harry Harrison's irreverant and dynamic satire *Bill the Galactic Hero*, which takes every aspect of pulp, fascist, Power-is-Truth sf war and milks them for their last drop of humour as it follows Bill's recruitment under the influence of a drink whose lacing of ego-reducing drug is so heavy that it is crystallising out in the bottom of the glass, to the final battle against

the reptilian Veniens. At the beginning of the book Bill comes under the awesome command of Petty Chief Officer Deathwish Drang:

'Right now you are nothing but horrible, sordid, flabby pieces of debased civilian flesh. I shall turn that flesh to muscle, your wills to jelly, your minds to machines. You will become good troopers, or I will kill you. Very soon you will be hearing stories about me, vicious stories about how I killed and ate a recruit who

disobeyed me.' He halted and stared at them, and slowly the coffin-lid lips parted in an evil travesty of a grin. 'That story is true!'

It is, of course, the weapons that make a war, rather than the numbers of men or *things*. Cultural disparity means technological disparity and that means an imbalance of weaponry—machine guns work well against clubs, but not if clubs are wielded by men in bullet-proof armour. Sf has always been fascinated by weaponry, the fact of weapons implying the dangerous nature of the environment, whether planetary or cosmic. A blaster must be strapped to the hip of every red-blooded true-human, or at least his digging tool must be able to double as a heat beam. When Jason Din Alt, in Harry Harrison's *Deathworld*, steps onto the surface of the planet Pyrrus he faces an organic environment so hostile that he must be able to draw his blaster quicker than the eye can see—the gun is rigged in his sleeve so that the slightest muscular twitch, neuronically indicating a need for self defence, presents the gun, ready-cocked, to his hand.

A different sort of weapon is the human mind. After all, if you can telekinete and teleport, you can make nonsense of physical projectiles. Richard Matheson's 'Witch War' is a graphic example of this. Seven little girls sit in a hut and 'think' mayhem

Soudot Cruiser Class *Also known as Inviolables, they were the most attractive of the bigger built Faberian craft. They included several desirable equipment developments, notably twin forward visual-sensory 'captivators' and a fully curved stern hull allowing maximum weapons energy excitement during rear attack.*

LEFT
Myriad Class Jetfighters *Human
close range, highly manoeuvrable
contact fighters, which could function
in atmosphere (withdrawing the
under and over gun implacements) or
in space. Limited to two days fire
power, and with a crew of only four
men, the fighters were invaluable in
small planetery disputes.*

RIGHT
Nimian Dreadnought, Time
Crashing *The briefly waged conflict
with the humanoid Nimians
resulted in a number of skirmishes
being fought during time
displacement, against all inter-
Empire agreements. Photographed
from a 'time sweeper', this
dreadnought was knocked back to
before the age of steam on Earth,
plunging into the sea after a time-
crash of over 4,000 years. The remains
were dredged by Time Haul and
Rescue Associates, who estimate over
a trillion New Dollars profit from the
operation.*

upon the invading armies. Their psychic powers, raw, immense, unstoppable, enable them to pound the enemy with boulders falling from the sky, or turn the ground to quagmire, or even just rend bodies as if some ferocious wild beast were tearing them. A more conventional weapon of war is the tank, the armoured mobile unit. Wells is credited with having thought up this particular horror, in his story 'The Land Ironclads', but his description of tank warfare is nowhere near as vivid as eye-witness accounts of the real tank war that occurred scant years later in World War I. Despite its human occupant, a tank is a robot, a machine of destruction that seems almost sentient as it pursues its enemy, a moving fortress, a metal-skinned creature capable of thought within limits, but most entirely capable of hideous destruction.

The sentient tank, or the sentient machine of war, frequently appears in sf. Fred Saberhagen's robot space ships, with their programmed destructive frenzy, are mentioned elsewhere in this book. Keith Laumer's short story 'The Last Command' describes an immense intelligent tank that is dug out of the rubble of the war in which it fought, and which instantly continues on its mission of death—it will obey only one man, the man who was once its human operator, but that man is now old and frail and his voice unrecognisable to the machine. Andrew Stephenson's Voyo in 'The Giant Killers' is an enemy tank that tracks down three soldiers in a jungle richly booby trapped with such unpleasant weapons as tackymat, which looks like a fresh cowpat but rapidly eats you alive, or rotspray that dissolves your flesh in seconds, not to mention other lovelies such as bindwort, jumping jack, misty eye, acid drop, and all manner of tiny robots—scarabs—each with a deadly comple-

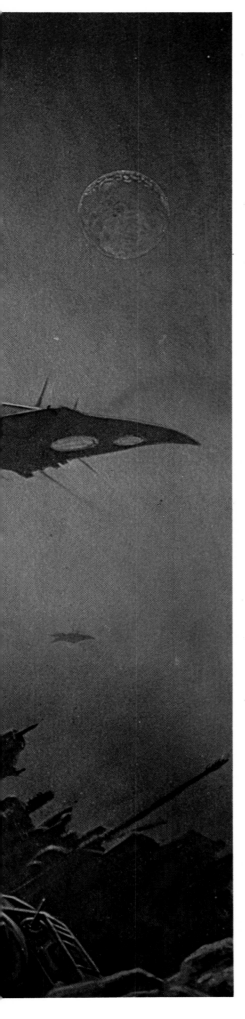

ment of weapons. The Voyo kills them one by one, as they run this awful gauntlet, in a horrible exercise in machine single-mindedness. Often, however, the machine of war began as a machine of peace, as in Ben Bova's *The Duelling Machine*; this is the perfect pacifier for all man's tensions, allowing an individual to enter a world of his own creation, destroy his enemy or be destroyed by him, and then emerge from his mental fantasy world completely unharmed—now someone has found a way to make use of this machine as a tool for destruction, and is using it to conquer a cluster of wealthy planetary systems.

Sometimes alien intervention can make a machine become a monster. In Theodore Sturgeon's 'Killdozer' a giant, highly complex, computer-programmed bulldozer smashes a boulder and releases the alien entity that is trapped therein; the alien locks into the bulldozers circuitry and goes berserk.

When it comes to war, though, only one machine can combine both mechanical mindlessness and human reason —the robot. Robots have stalked future battlefields for as long as they have stalked the pages of science fiction— gigantic robots, or tiny scurrying robots, they combine all the good and desirable qualities of a human soldier— they don't question, they obey without hesitation, they do not feel fear, or pain, and can go that much further towards the enemy before they are finally brought down. They can sometimes get their positronic brain circuits addled by shell shock, however, as in Walter Miller's 'I Made You' where the army robot has turned against its own human controller, has trapped him in a cave and is waiting for the flimsy human to make a break for it as starvation affects his reason—and then it will laser him down. In Philip K. Dick's 'Second Variety' a soldier runs the gauntlet of tiny, vicious robot weapons as he seeks escape from the battlefield:

Quarix Weapons Function Robot
An elusive race, the reptiliaform Quarix fashioned these bizarre robots after their young forms, adding wheels to enable the machines to traverse any blasted or ruined wasteland with more ease. The robots were designed not to destroy intelligent life, but other robots were, especially the small, scurrying forms that tend to remain undiscovered and fatally operational on battlegrounds after the Second Interregnum.

Across the ground something small and metallic came flashing in the dull sunlight of midday. A metal sphere. It raced up the hill . . . it's treads flying. It was small, one of the baby ones. Its claws were out, two razor projections spinning in a blur of white steel.

The automatic factories, programmed for war production, have taken over completely and are producing robots of different varieties at an ever increasing rate. When they start mimicking not just human beings, but individual human beings, the war against them is as good as lost. Philip K. Dick was one of the most energetic of science fiction writers in the 50s and 60s, continually, almost obsessively, exploring themes of identity and automation. His robot stories reflect the growing insecurity of that period with the idea that machine identity was a necessary, almost inevitable, adjunct of increasing computer complexity. When a man is reflected precisely in metal, and the metal can think like the man, the distinction between man and machine becomes blurred. His story 'Imposter' brilliantly analyses this problem. Spence Olham has returned to the domed city that is his home to find he is suspected of being an enemy robot in Olham's image, sent to infiltrate the terrestrial city. The intelligence rumour is that the Olham-robot contains a tiny, planet-busting bomb that will trigger if it speaks certain code words. Olham desperately tries to prove he isn't the robot, and eventually finds the crashed remains of his personal ship with the robot inside that indeed *has* been sent to infiltrate the city. Only the remains are not of a robot at all, they are human remains. Olham stares at them aghast and says, 'But if that's Olham, then I'm . . .' and the resulting explosion was visible all the way to Alpha Centauri! Garry Kilworth's Colonel 607, in 'The Soul Of Colonel 607' is a robot officer commanding a robot force during a land-based battle; but it/he has become aware of itself and of the ethical considerations of war. When your robot troops start to question orders, there is only one thing to do—repair them!

Robots, created in man's image and described in science fiction, are literary playthings akin to a child's playing with dolls or models, a manipulable non-real form into which and onto which a writer can project his ideas. Like marionettes the metal men have been dragged through the pages of science

fiction at a writer's whim and gradually a certain control has been acquired over the strings of the puppets. The robot is a mirror in which the writer can reflect something of the human philosopher's eternal quest for the roots of human behaviour, and more importantly, as the question of awareness arises, into the roots of human thought and 'identity'.

At a stroke of genius, in the early 1940s, Isaac Asimov took the concept of the robot and transformed it from the clanking, monstrous, unpredictable, unreasoned and inadequately conceived plot element that it was, into a real functional tool, at once a prediction of what a machine might one day become, and a symbol of what man may have been in his evolutionary dawn. Asimov invented the laws of robotics, three simple, elegant laws: that a robot

should not injure, or harm or kill humans, nor disobey them unless that contradicted the first law, nor allow itself to come to harm, unless again that contradicted the preceding laws. Now the concept of the robot became that of a programmed and programmable tool, something that could be ordered to do any job within its capability, but which had an underlying 'ethical' programme that for ever would keep it from the battlefield, or from harming its master, or from being used as a weapon. But the laws are ambiguous, as ambiguous in their way as is human nature. To tell a robot to 'get lost' ('Little Lost Robot') is an instruction that will be taken literally with near disastrous results; a robot will prevent a man crossing a dangerous road (as in Jack Williamson's 'With Folded Hands') and even more subtly

Desert Warfare on Arrakis
Duneworld was the site of several inter-Empire skirmishes, usually held far away from the areas of denser human population, and beyond the range of the sandworms and Fremen raiders. Here the desert tanks of two Earth National Planetary Enterprises (thought to be US Starpushers Inc. & All African Stimulants Co.) face up for a 'contest' to decide the outcome of an industrial dispute.

it will lie to a man, as in Asimov's 'Liar', when it knows that the truth of a particular situation will cause a man grief, and so 'harm' him.

Asimov's robot stories reach both a series and evolutionary climax with the award winning, and quite brilliant novella, 'The Bicentennial Man'. Now at last Asimov asks the questions that he has broached and skirted around in all the previous stories—what *is* a man? The robot of the story is old, and is continually repaired, and many of the repairs keeping it effectively immortal are organic replacements. Soon it is more organic than many rich men who have kept themselves alive with inorganic transplants and prosthetics. Which is the more human? The robot is extraordinarily aware. Finally it asks, does it matter whether a mind is fashioned from the womb or the workbench? Surely the fact of the mind's existence is all that matters, and if that mind is in the human mould, then can it not be called human?

DreadHulk *The DreadHulks were six alien machines—probably from the early now extinct Vegan Principality—that were found in working order in a deep crystal installation on the radioactive planet known as Barmstoke's World. Reequipped with ultra strong Wingrove crawler tracks, their inexplicable weapons replaced with Carlsen 20cm split violators and Morgan-Dungate scan beam weapons couplings, the dreadHulks were used in action against the Belegenian uprising on the city worlds of Kryptos and Hickenlooper's Planet. Each machine was possessed of a rudimentary intelligence and was capable of taking reasoned action of its own. They functioned as transporters for smaller mobile armoured machines and for troops— capacity 5,000 men, plus equipment. Whole sections and levels of the dreadHulks were never penetrated and the machines committed a form of self destruction 30 years after being discovered.*

Fantastic Creatures

'... enigmatic life form that is abused, misused, loved and an object of fun'

Stamping on toads is not a sociable thing to do, especially if the toad is an intelligent visitor from Proxima Centauri. If they're tourists, that's a slightly different matter, but they may be emissaries. The galaxy is a big place and a weird place—all too often it's a repulsive place, but man must take a strong hold on his stomach and face the variformed creatures from the stars with a smile on his face. Somewhere in the universe, that undulating jelly creature has a mother; and that giant slug that smears you with fetid slime is merely conveying its respects. Put away that blaster, Carstairs, that crab creature has an IQ of one million.

Whether abused, misused, explored with love and care or made into an object of fun, the alien being has been a challenge for the creative sf writer or artist. Unfortunately, it is all too easy to take a serious attempt at depicting the life of another world and turn it into an image of the ridiculous. Public reaction is unpredictable. Some audiences collapse into hysterical laughter as the twee little aliens enter at the end of *Close Encounters of the Third Kind*, and yet the parody aliens in *Star Wars* receive enormous praise and are taken almost seriously. When Fred Brown wrote the memorable 'Arena', in which a human competes against a small, blobby alien for his own life and the life of his world, the alien simplicity of the story left an image of terror; but when the story was adapted for *Star Trek*, and the alien became a bipedal alligator with a bad case of indigestion, audiences broke up.

The problem is the same in sf art. The early pulp magazines invariably used the alien entity in a dramatically hostile role; those covers pulse with dynamism, every muscle strains in the human characters, every stroke of the brush is used to effect excitement. What were the audience reactions at the time, one wonders? Did all those fangs, tentacles, enormous eyes, scaly bodies and malicious intentions reach the chords of fear in those who picked them up? They seem so hopelessly naive

now, ineffective, unrealistic. The most effective aliens in science fiction— with exceptions—remain those that were difficult to illustrate. There is something horrifyingly memorable about the tiny aliens in Robert Silverberg's 'Passengers', who take over human bodies and use them in all manner of grotesque ways; Heinlein's aliens in *The Puppet Masters* are slugs that tap into the human spinal cord to control their hosts; Terry Carr's aliens in 'The Dance Of The Changer And The Three' are almost wholly energy forms, their consciousness coalescing around a single point in space, their visible form anything from a tiny spiral to a snowflake. Almost impossible to imagine, hugely difficult to draw, they are perfect symbols of the ultimate gulf that can separate life forms.

Another enigmatic alien life form is in Stanislaw Lem's *Solaris*, a world covered by an ocean that is a single gigantic, telepathic organism which traps the spirits and souls of the humans orbiting about it, and eventually becomes a surrogate world for them. Another mind-boggling and virtually unillustrable alien is the planet-wide nervous system in Ursula K. LeGuin's 'Vaster Than Empires And More Slow', and yet it is one of the most fantastic creatures ever imagined.

Jovian Medusoid *Indigenous life form of Jupiter, the medusoid-type creature is over a thousand spans in diameter. It drifts in the middle layer of the Jovian atmosphere, gaining energy from high stratosphere electric storms. It browses on organic molecules excreted by smaller, non-intelligent life forms. Contact was made early in space history by astronauts in small capsules suspended by heavy weather balloons such as those shown here.*

Yet those pulp covers with their all too palpable monsters continue to fascinate the sf fan, collector and true student. Who can doubt that Wesso's (Hans Wessolowski) incorrigibly vicious aliens, with their gigantic heads and bulging, fish-like eyes, were the original little green men that have become such a potent symbol of the anti-intellectual attitude to sf? They appear everywhere, those malicious little beasts, riding their space machines, taking undoubted pleasure in destroying sundry items of Americana, bottling and dissecting human wenches in flimsy attire, or bursting through doors scattering death rays in all directions. Only rarely did a cover feature an alien engaged in

some sort of gentle cooperation with humanity and it is quite noticeable that whenever such fraternisation occurred, the alien was usually male, and differed from the rugged human male stereotype only in having an acceptably neutral skin colour, such as purple. If he was green he was inevitably violent and mad; black . . . well, that was *totally* unacceptable, as was red, at least on humanoid aliens who could conceivably have been superior to the true humans. Of course, not all the old magazines were catering to such a low denominator, and even within runs of the same magazines the occasional lapse into taste can be detected. However, on the whole aliens that were manifestly not men in purple skin-suits were there to

Tropemen *Bizarre humanoid alien species, the Tropemen are restricted almost entirely to their evolutionary homeworld, Trope. Their crystal eyes are more than light sensitive, though their full subsensory range is not yet known. Their telepathic ability is highly advanced. The Federation recruits young Tropemen for service monitoring natural stargates.*

menace woman, to be shot at by men, and to give the horrifying impression that true grit and mere bullets alone would not stop them; they would thunder on regardless, tentacles, fangs, claws and drool taking their toll of innocent human life.

Gigantism too became a symbol of horror. The giant man in a scaly skin, busily engaged in wrenching apart some bridge or other (or is he repairing it?) conforms to the human-as-alien pattern, but his vast size, and obvious affinity with the fish world, marks him clear enough as not being on our side. Such mindlessness of intent, all energy channelled towards attack, destroy, kidnap, and then . . . then what?

The point has often been raised, by those cynical enough to question what is going on behind the scenes, just why *are* those green-skinned aliens, or those clawed, scaly sub-reptilians, trying so hard to get the woman? What are they going to do with her—eat her? Or perhaps the shuddering truth is that they wish to 'interfere' with them. Can there be any doubt at all that that is the true intention of all pulp aliens, that in their search for universal knowledge

LEFT
Faberian Emperor Je'kirioth *The Emperior lying in state on the ghost world Spectre B, after his assassination by an army faction. This was later destroyed by antirepublican troops and non-military inhabitants of the capital city, Kurix. Of the rarely seen thorn caste, Je'kirioth was considered to have been one of the greatest of the Faberian emperors, and with his death the first strain between the Terran and Faberian Empires became apparent as his policy of non-contest over border worlds was gradually eroded.*

LEFT
Zoni Warrior from Jaimbaliz *Contested by both Thangan and Terran Federations because of its natural oil wealth (and its place on the edge of the Lyran system), Jaimbaliz was saved by its native military forces. Technically naive and equipped only with primitive explosive capsule guns, they nonetheless managed to defeat two land-based factions from each would-be overlord race. The Terran Empire made formal amends and signed a treaty of trade alignment.*

Delaney's World *In the system of Beta Dhalgren, Delaney's World boasts semi-intelligent life, the gigantic reptiliaforms known as torons. Human colonists have formed symbiotic relationships with the creatures, similar to the man-dragon relationship on the nearby world of Pern.*

offspring, for the way of things is that the young's first meal is its mother.

In recent years the fantastic creature has dropped quite substantially out of science fiction cover art. The artist's fetish for depicted the fantastic future is now the gadget, usually a space ship, often a sprawling, wonderfully detailed city. However two artist in particular, Kelly Freas and John Schoenherr retain their always very substantial interest in painting aliens, and they continue to depict exquisitely the alien characters of stories that, regrettably, are far less memorable. Schoenherr has excelled at painting the planet Arrakis for Frank Herbert's *Dune* books, including the gigantic, semi-sentient sandworms that are so important to the ecology of the world. He has also been the most impressive artist linked with Anne McCaffrey's wonderful sequence of tales about the planet Pern, notably *Dragonflight*. Pern is an alien world that is to the Dark Ages what most fantasy is to Medieval Europe; it is a world of defended Holds, usually built on high ground, that take their resources from an area of rural land bordering vast areas of virgin terrain across which hostile bands from other Holds move in search of conquest. It is evocatively drawn and wonderfully described, particularly the bizarre symbiosis that the human inhabitants of Pern share with the native sentient life form, giant, dragonlike, gentle creatures. Little threatens them, but whenever Pern drifts close to its sister planet, one of the strangest invasions from another world occurs, as silvery, intelligent 'threads' move across space and penetrate the atmosphere of the Dragon World.

Gentle, intelligent aliens account for at least two more memorable species in the fantastic future of sf. They are the Nildoror of Robert Silverberg's seminal novel *Downward to the Earth*, and the Lithians from James Blish's *A Case of Conscience*, which have rarely been drawn with any imagination and are usually depicted as dinosaurs. Yet the Lithians are a fascinating example of how a skilled writer can explore themes basic to the human conception and perception of the universe—in this case, the true nature of religious belief —and still create an exciting and believable alien world. The Lithians, for all that they are intelligent, benevolent, fully aware of their place in the scheme of things, and totally given to an existence founded on the same under-

they require carnal knowledge of human females? Horrible indeed, whereas the reverse is rarely so nauseating. John Carter makes love to a bevy of lovely Martian princesses, and that's alright with everyone. Those Martian princesses, though! They really are quite alien, despite looking remarkably like over-inflated Raquel Welch dolls. Alien breasts, bottoms and thighs leave humanoid observers weak at the knees, but the alienness is undoubtedly there —they lay eggs, after all!

But it doesn't always work as cosily as on Barsoom. The human male in Philip José Farmer's precedent-setting 'The Lovers' makes love to, impregnates, and becomes emotionally tangled with a lovely alien female, an alien in impossibly human form, who is subsequently eaten alive by her hybrid

standing of social responsibility, are totally without any conception of god or original sin. The ethical problem they pose to the religion-orientated human visitors is one of the great explorations of science fiction, and *A Case of Conscience* is one of the great but generally underrated novels of the last 20 years.

The Nildoror of Robert Silverberg's novel are somewhat akin to the terrestrial elephant, but only somewhat. Theirs is a world of forest, jungle and high mountains across which they

Death and Water Ritual among the Grillka'shanaskilk *This intelligent reptiliaform species, indigenous to the waterworld Magog IV, has a complex death ritual involving the retention of fluid in their bodies until their tissues literally swell to fluid balloons. This female 'queen' (egg laying as opposed to egg hatching) is in the third Terran month of the ritual and is close to death.*

migrate at regular intervals. They are peaceful and peaceable and horribly exploited by the human colonists of the place, who use them as pack animals. A second race of alien/natives, the Sulidoror, are very different, being upright and aggressive. The relationship between the two species is complex and grotesque and it is the discovery of this that is one theme of the book, a metaphor for the more complex self discovery that an Earthman undergoes as he risks his universal integrity to try an alien drug.

Just as certain aliens are memorable for the skill with which an author has drawn them or an artist has painted them, so certain writers are memorable for their alien-types. One can almost categorise them. A Clifford Simak alien is small, helpless, discovered lurking in the bushes somewhere in middle America and will communicate its distress telepathically; an A. E. van Vogt alien will have been trapped on a strange world, or in an enormous alien construct, for millions of years, and is waiting only for some hapless human to release it; a Christopher Anvil, Eric Frank Russell or early Robert Silverberg alien is basically humanoid, technologically very advanced, intellectually a bit naive, has no sense of humour, no conception of human con-artistry or greed, and naturally falls foul of both; a Ray Bradbury alien is slender, fragile, part of an ancient race, totally without original sin and immensely susceptible to human aggression; an E. E. 'Doc'

Smith alien is invariably dead; an Arthur Clarke alien is hugely old, incredibly wise (even enigmatic) and arrives on long-devastated earth only to end up watching Walt Disney cartoons; Tanith Lee aliens are invariably female humanoids, use undirty dirty words and enjoy having the gates of their citadels breached by the hero's battering ram.

Humanoid aliens abound in science fiction, perhaps painted more human than the author meant to imply. To evolve, quite distinctly to *homo sapiens*, a race identical down to the joints of the finger (if not skin colour) has caused many a biologist to tear his hair. Creatures that combine all the lesser qualities of slugs, crabs and octopoids are similarly infuriating, especially when they are described or shown as living in incompatible environments. But if the bug-eyed monster is out of fashion, the humanoid alien certainly isn't. Silverberg, again, in *Those Who Watch* has three aliens crashed on our world and tended for in different ways by three inhabitants of the more deserted reaches of New Mexico. Michael Bishop's *Funeral for the Eyes of Fire* introduces us to the Tropemen, humanoid aliens with bizarre crystal eyes and tremendous telepathic powers; the artist Melvyn has captured them well in his cover painting for the book. Classic among the humanoid aliens are Zenna Henderson's The People, who hide away in a deep box valley on Earth to avoid any interference with the populace of the world. Far removed, ethically and in their intent, are Keith Laumer's shape changing aliens in *A Plague of Demons*, who assume human form with conquest in mind.

The strange aliens in Ursula K. LeGuin's *The Word for World is Forest* spend much of their lives dreaming, and their dreamworld is as real as the forest environment of the planet, already being overrun by insensitive humans. Although the aliens are humanoid, LeGuin is far more concerned with the alienness of spirit than body and where a writer's concern is this, it would be madness not to establish a reader identification with the alien form. The truly memorable alien Gethenians, from the *Left Hand of Darkness*, are humanoid too and the hermaphrodite, snow bound, the Gethenian society and lifestyle is brilliantly worked out.

Kurt Vonnegut uses aliens for a very different reason: satire. Like many other writers, he is less concerned with the

Chameleon *One of the results of illegal tampering with genetics and the crossbreeding of species was the production of a population of bizarre creatures known variously as Chameleons, Leos and Scorps. Their function was to have been to guard estates and plantations on the fertile worlds in the Crowley System of 27 Earth-type (−17 to +48 on the Croot Comparison Scale) worlds, but their intelligence and compassion led to them being seeded on a world of their own, Lioness, orbiting the yellow sun Panox B.*

fact of the alien as with its symbolic use. The creatures that inhabit Titan, in his superbly funny *The Sirens of Titan*, are alien whether they are human or Tralfamadorian; Salo, the true alien, is a short, three-legged creature, with a round head hung on gimbals and a skin the colour and texture of an Earthling tangerine—he is eleven million years old. He inhabits Titan with doomed Earthman Malachi Constant, and occasionally with the bizarre Winston Rumfoord, who is caught up in a chronosynclastic infundibulum, which means he pulses around the universe in distorted spirals, materialising on any physical body he intercepts. Vonnegut's intent is always to isolate, analyse and satirise microcosms of human life; his Tralfamadorians kidnap Billy Pilgrim and the luscious starlet, Montana Wildhack and set them up in a zoo, a typical modern day lounge, protected by a dome from the volcanic, steaming wastes of the planet. The Tralfamadorians are true swamis, able to see

both the future and the past at the same time, so that death is meaningless for them, being merely one continuing event in a rich tapestry of life events that they can enjoy *ad infinitum*.

Larry Niven has made his name for his stories dealing with known space, a galaxy sufficiently unexplored to retain mystery, yet sufficiently explored for Niven to populate his fiction with all manner of strange alien beings, from the knobby, beaked, immensely powerful Protector, who seeds worlds with food and later harvests it (Earth being a seed world, we being the harvest) to the truly memorable Pierson's Puppeteers, extremely cowardly creatures, tripedal, two-headed, and very gentle and intelligent indeed. His humans too have a tendency to be strange, notably Teela Brown from *Ringworld* who has been genetically bred for luck. With Jerry Pournelle, Niven created the mammoth mystery of *The Mote in God's Eye*, an interstellar space ship that has taken eons to reach known space, and which is evacuated

62

of all life within moments of its achieving contact with the human empire. The quest for the Moties begins, their life forms and lifestyles are slowly suggested, and the link between the social castes in their termite-like social structure is finally revealed.

Earth has been invaded over and over again. The classics are Wells' *The War of the Worlds* and Wyndham's *The Day of the Triffids*. Wells' book describes the arrival of the fleshy, spindle-limbed Martians who are only comfortable when riding their huge, tripedal war machines. To them, humans are just cattle, useful for their blood and for having tamed much of the earth and made it suitable for the Martians to occupy. Wyndham's triffids are alien plants, grown from seeds that have drifted through interstellar space. When a catastrophe strikes the whole world blind, the triffids—intelligent creatures who have disguised this fact well—decide that it is time to start taking over. Three-legged, motile plant-life, they possess a fatal sting and a horrifying ability to multiply at a fantastic rate. In *The Kraken Wakes*, a rather ineffective novel, Wyndham has the Earth invaded by carapaced monsters from the deep, but his *The Midwich Cuckoos*, with its invasion directly into the genes and wombs of terrestrial women, is a classic and a brilliant notion with all its subtle Christian irony: the virgin birth of something greater than man, which in this instance is very much an Antichrist. Here it is the human children themselves who are alien, a concept and a projection that is as frightening as the invisible possessor of the body in Hal Clement's *Needle*, for example, where the never-seen alien is lodged in a human boy and communicates by directly tapping into his optic nerve so that he *sees* the alien speech.

Human beings as aliens has been taken further and there are two notable stories, built on an identical theme. In Ray Bradbury's 'Dark They Were And Golden Eyed' human colonists on ancient Mars find life on the grasslands, bordering the dried seas and crumbling cities of the dead Martians increasingly idyllic; they begin to speak strange words; their eyes become golden, their skins brown. When an expedition from Earth arrives generations later, they find a race of Martians but no trace of the original human colonists. In A. E. van Vogt's 'Enchanted Village' a marooned Earth astronaut crawls into a

ruined Martian town, is nurtured and nourished by it as it once, millions of years before, nourished the original inhabitants. Ultimately his form changes as he rapidly adapts to the village, and the world, and eventually he transmutes into a replica of the life that once lived there.

In Robert Silverberg's *Thorns* and *The Man in the Maze* a male character appears who has been altered by aliens in such a way that he is now deeply and totally repugnant to members of his own species; this was an interesting turn for Silverberg's continuing study of the nature of alienness. In Frederik Pohl's *Man Plus* an astronaut has been so extensively biologically modified, in order to adapt him to conditions on Mars, that he can no longer be considered fully human, with a resultant awful psychological effect upon him. Isaac Asimov has explored man as alien from the robot point of view, making his robots more and more intelligent, self aware, and even or-

Necromancer This world, in the Black Suns Zone, on the fringe of Faberian dominated space, was terraformed during the Second Empire, but with disastrous results. The world, called Necromancer because of the immense alien graveyard that was discovered there containing some 400 million separate stone coffins, was in fact a 'waiting place', the coffins being a strange and incomprehensible suspended animation system. The world was called haunted because the waiting aliens destroyed every attempt to colonise it, as shown in this nightview taken by robot-eye. The creatures, intelligent, vicious, uncommunicative beings, are known as Greegs.

ganic, so that eventually, in 'The Bicentennial Man' a robot questions why, being comprised of more human organ components than a lot of humans themselves, it is still a robot.

Solar system life is what mostly preoccupies the science fiction writer, moreso in the past than today, it's true, but there remains a healthy interest, and a healthy belief; those elusive Martian bacteria not quite, but almost, discovered by Viking have in no way diminished the intrinsic belief that somewhere around our G-type sun there exists intelligent life apart from man. There are certainly no moon-calves herded by insectoidal Selenites during the long lunar day, before being taken below into atmosphere-filled caverns while the moon's air freezes during the long night; yet it is impossible to read Wells' *The First Men in the Moon* without casting wistful glances at our pockmarked sibling world. There may be no curvaceous maidens on Mars or Venus but organic traces have been found on meteorites, so a devastating virus invasion, as brilliantly described in Michael Crichton's *The Andromeda Strain*, is always a possibility. The outer planets, vast Jupiter and Saturn, mysterious Neptune, exotic Uranus and frozen Pluto, all of these worlds may contain the wasted, devastated, ammonia-racked remains of civilisations, but more likely life there will be of the basic survival type, adapted to its hostile environment, and limited in any spiritual or intellectual development to something so outside our carbon/water mentality that it can be only hinted at.

Arthur Clarke's award winning story 'A Meeting with Medusa' evokes the desperate distance between worlds, and between different forms of life. The medusoid creature that rises and sinks through the dense hydrocarbon clouds of Jupiter, its tentacles absorbing energy and nutriment, its intelligence hinted at by its baffled but recognisable curiosity about the balloon-supported space vehicle that is descending through the cloud layers, is so real because it derives from how things are known to be, and in its own way it is as romantic, as exciting, as the rain forests of red hot Venus, and at the other the Martian bacteria that everybody just *knows* are lurking beneath the desert, waiting for the start of the Martian summer that still lies years away by our standards.

FAR LEFT
Mesklinites *Centipedal, intelligent, friendly creatures from the discus-shaped world Mesklin, the Mesklinites were used extensively by the Human expeditionary forces in the early Empire to explore worlds too hostile for man.*

LEFT
Sandworm *Indigenous animal species on Arrakis, or Dune, a planet famous for its natural drug product* melange. *The sandworm is enormous, but can be controlled by men as it has a rudimentary intelligence. Its maw is hundreds of yards across and many an unsuspecting sand vehicle has been swallowed by these creatures, attracted to the surface of the drum sands by the engine vibration. Even a man's footfall can attract the beasts.*

LEFT
War of the Worlds *A classic for over five millennia, H. G. Wells's imaginary story of an invasion by Martians in tripedal war machines still excites younger readers. Even by Zone War standards the vicious and almost mindless vision of the Martian subjugation of the Human race is terrifying.*

Fantasy

'. . . future fiction deals with all human life, its societies and cultures'

There are those who say that sf is adolescent in its approach to sex and fantasy, but fantasy represents only one part of the broad and varied *schema* of fantastic fiction, a fiction where the setting of fantastic/future societies is now being used increasingly to delve into human-kind's sexuality.

There may not be sex after death—at least, not conventional sex—but if the visions of the science fiction writers are anything to go by then there will most certainly be sex—mostly unconventional sex—until the bitter end of time. Running in parallel with the so-called rise in free thinking and free love, sf jerked itself into adolescence and found that sex was a very good subject to explore in futuristic/technological terms. Edward Bellamy, in the 19th century book *Looking Backward* and others, managed to shock his readers with his utopian visions of love, a free and easy society love un-rammelled by morality or censorship. Sixty years later the same fixation with open marriage and unquestioned sexual exchange crops up in the fiction time after time. These days it is far more explicit. Only 20 years ago hard-core sf fans would have spluttered into their milk at the idea of science fiction dealing with the future of fornication, and regrettably the act and the design have always been confused, almost until the 1970s. The fact that sex means no more than an intraspecies relationship, founded on certain complex ethical, social and biological laws, was too hard to grasp. If a book was reviewed as a 'soft science fiction' book, dealing with human relationships, including their sexual relationships, then it was condemned in certain circles as pulsating with filth and unnatural acts. This happened extensively in the 1960s in Britain as the 'New Wave' of speculative fiction tried desperately to show that future fiction, like all fiction, dealt with 'all human life', that there were no unnatural acts save those imposed by culture, and cultures differ, and that to be constrained by unwritten laws governing the science and specu-

lative fiction tried desperately to sf writers were, and regrettably still are—was to constrain not just imagination, but also talent, values and the emotional energy required to produce true fiction. But then, when a black and white picture of a man standing with his index finger raised can draw letters of protest from a magazine's

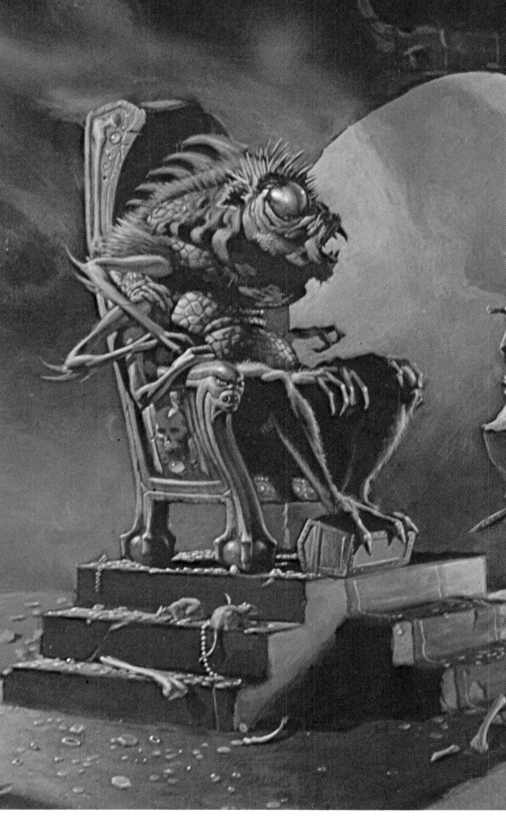

ABOVE
Tanash *The grotesque Lord of the Thark-dominated world of Nibonez. Human colonists on the world have reverted to sword-carrying primitives and cannot match their overlords for magical ability.*

readership, the time is obviously not right to try anything too ambitious.

The chains of unreason still imprison many otherwise excellent minds; little has changed, save the fictional explicitness, since the early 1950s, when Philip José Farmer's story 'The Lovers' appeared. What an incredibly naive myth has grown up around this rather mediocre story. It has been hailed time and time again as 'the breakthrough' in sf, the first small step for a man, the first giant leap for the sub-genre. Sex had come to science fiction, and with it the first wispy bristles of adulthood. Yet the story is about a man who impregnates an alien woman and whose resulting offspring consume her. All the heavy breathing takes place behind a row of dots. Theodore Sturgeon was treading far more 'dangerous' ground, exploring themes of sexual frustration and homosexuality.

The confusion between physical and emotive love has haunted sf always, but now at last there is at least a balance. Stories may deal unnecessarily, and rather grotesquely, with the mechanics of lubricant-assisted piston-action, but the relationship of sex to technological and hybrid-cultural evolution is the main concern. Brian Aldiss, for example, has examined the problem of sex in a society where physical contact has been reduced practically to zero. In 'Three Songs For Enigmatic Lovers' he points out that if you can see who you like when you like as a solid, apparently real presence in your room (holographic projection) the question must be asked, can two holograph images make love? The answer

is no. But Robert Silverberg's 'In The Group' explores the way technology may be able to allow us a share in the emotional and physical sex of others, and even how whole groups of people may be able to make love to the same person at the same time, sharing everything through a neuronic link-up to the single person in action. Naturally a problem arises from this, and Silverberg as only Silverberg can, analyses and complicates the fact of one man who no longer wishes to share the sensory group-feast, but to keep his woman to himself.

This sort of fiction, graphic yet reasoned, exploring and interpreting in a meaningful way, seems a class apart from the deliberate pornographic fantasy of Philip José Farmer's *The Image of the Beast, Blown* and *A Feast Unknown.* Farmer may, in many people's eye, have opened the crack that led to the breaking of the sex taboo in sf, but what can those same people think of a book concerned virtually solely with a man being sexually 'pleasured' in every known way by a woman with a very strange anatomy indeed? In *Blown* a character with the name of Childe (can there be some symbolic irony here?) discovers a woman called Vivienne who has a long, active snake-like creature living in her womb. Childe soon comes under the spell of Vivienne and indulges in orgy after orgy with her gorgeous friends—all the time he is discovering, piece by piece, that Vivienne is alien, from the Andromeda galaxy no less. As the tension increases, and the story moves inexorably towards the ultimate

rape upon Childe's body so he experiences strange things during a bizarre orgiastic ritual, seeing 'flashes of the exotic and extra-terrestrial landscapes' whenever he is being sexually stimulated.

While all this is meaningless trivia, other writers, not afraid of throwing their experiential and descriptive punches, are exploring all manner of futures for the most important instinctive behaviour of man. A. K. Jorgensson's hideous vision 'Coming Of Age Day' is of a future where population is controlled by equipping each boy and girl at puberty with a 'consex', a unisex organic fitting that is like an inbuilt member of the opposite sex. This allows sexual pleasure as and when its wanted, but eliminates 'social' diseases and unwanted babies. The alarming prosthesis is 'only ordinary flesh. It has a tiny pulse with a primitive sort of heart, and blood and muscle. And fat. It's just flesh. Alive, of course, but perfectly harmless.'

Many envisioned futures are futures without men. How are they viable? If not by the use of sperm banks then hermaphroditism has arisen, or parthenogenesis. John Wyndham eliminated men in 'Consider Her Ways' by the use of a potent rat poison, and his female character has a vision of the terrifying future where she is just a breeding machine, a great bloated cow of a woman producing girl children. Joanna Russ took a space ship of women to the planet Whileaway and developed their all-female culture, exploring the basis of role separation and allocation in our own society. In 'When

The Hordes of Thark *Pursued by winged 'harpies', malevolent robot soldiers of the Thark Lord, a Human sweating in a replica of an early armoured suit, rides from the 'challenge' the ritual contesting of Human rights.*

The Gates of Ivrel *Built by an unknown and long dead alien race, these stone gates are thru ways which perforate the galaxy, ancient matter transmitters. Their destinations are not known. Defending this particular gate are its guardians, fearsome warriors called Cherryhs.*

It Changed' her point is that most behavioural secondary sexual characteristics are learned rather than innate. Role playing is dictated by society and culture, and yet the paradox is that a patriarchal society is stronger and more stable—on the evidence of the world!—than a matriarchal society. The human males who visit Whileaway ask the inevitable question as they face a population of women trained in hundreds of different ways—mechanics to cleaners—'which of you plays the man's role?'. And the question is beautifully ironic in its sexual ambiguity.

In James Tiptree's astonishing story 'Houston, Houston, Do You Read?' a small space capsule, crewed by men, is jacked into the future by some disturbance in the fabric of space. Here they meet up with a capsule staffed solely by women. Men, it seems, have all died by this time in the future and the sperm banks are getting low. The time-lost are a God given opportunity to replenish the banks, but first the old techniques of sex have to be relearned; and as this happens so the differences between men become clear as the male

astronauts settle into a pecking order or dominance from the aggressive cock-sure type who contemplates the millions of women that are his and his alone, to the quiet, wiser type who comprehends the danger they are in, because of course culturally and socially they are dangerous to the women and cannot be allowed to survive.

Humankind reduced to one sex is one vision of the future which makes for social complications, but the reverse is also true. In his obscure but brilliant novel *Son of Man* Robert Silverberg explores worlds of reality and unreality, slipping easily from one to the other so that the reader is caught up in a progression of adventures and images that reflect and illuminate one another, the whole journey becoming a moving and arousing exploration towards the recognition of the subtle and complex creature that is man. Clay, the only recognisably human character, awakes in the far distant future at a time when humanity has diversified into so many forms that mankind has become an entire ecosystem. The sensual, aggressive, emotional and rational facets of the human psyche are now delineated

71

RIGHT
The Grave of Nig Bvean *The discovery of the resting place of this ancient, one-armed explorer of some of the lesser worlds in the Dark Zone of the galaxy. The Federation Health Agency sent several expeditions in search of the enigmatic and crippled spaceace who had boozed his way through a thousand worlds after discovering the secret of eternal life. They came too late. The secret potion had run out and Nig, a surprised man, had died.*

BELOW
Stonehenge *On the planet known as Harrison's World humanoid culture was discovered at a level of development approximating to the Terran Bronze Age. Their immense stone structures, called henges, suggest some connection or contact with primitive Earth.*

within their own human forms, gross creatures all, straight cut of Fellini, though some slip into and out of forms as easily as they make love to Clay in this time where, as they laughingly point out, sex is obsolete as anything but an historical plaything. Our hero is lured by a sextet of naiads who sexually titivate him in an idyllic pool. 'Someone explores his armpit. Someone enters his ear. "Enough!" he splutters, but they continue awhile. Finally he arises, wearing an awkward erection and clambers to the shore, finding all six of them male and laughing.'

As a complete contrast in both idea and ethic, not to mention approach, John Sladek has produced many stories that deal satirically with the machine dominated future. He has realised quite quickly that intelligent machines will also have a sex drive and his exercise in steel seduction, 'Machine Screw', illustrates the point well, as a gigantic laboratory robot-machine breaks loose to scour the countryside seeking sexual satisfaction. It achieves momentary satiation by raping a cadillac (to the horror of the two humans in the back seat) but finds a readymade orgy as the generals send in the tanks to destroy it.

Sladek's slapstick humour, illuminating many of the pretensions of the modern day sf writers who declare so fervently that they and their fiction are 'dangerous', contrasts perfectly with the subtle, almost subliminal, sexual exploration of Fred Pohl's *Gateway*. Ostensibly a novel about man's use of a deserted alien space station, equipped with star ships whose destinations are pre-designated but never known, it is more deeply about man's universal impotence, and the hero's specifically sexual impotence in particular. The novel charts our hero's experiences with sex and space stations, while reporting on his long-time-later analysis sessions with a computer psychiatrist. Suffice it to say that part of the problem revolves around the largest womb-destroyer symbol in the universe, a Black Hole.

If science fiction can be seen to be maturing in both its attitude to 'sex', and to the role of women in the stories, and indeed to women writers, the same cannot be said of fantastic art. A book or magazine cover, it must be understood, is part of the selling process, not part of the creative process, and as such it must cater for a different sort of fantasy than the imaginative fantasy of the fiction. It must provoke an instant sense of excitement, or enthralled wonder, or it must appeal to the ideotypic adolescent that lives on, whatever a reader's age—it must hit him where he is most susceptible, giving him a promise of wide open spaces, whether universal or sexual. In the grand days of the pulp magazines women appeared rarely in the stories, save as harem cattle, or helpless virgin girls threatened either by aliens or the powermaniacs who ruled the galaxy. On the covers they appeared similarly helpless, but usually far more scantily clad. Flip through a pile of pulp magazines and see proof that man in the male sense is overwhelmingly at the mercy of his gonads, and thinks of himself as positive to a woman's negative, decisive to her trembling helplessness, square shouldered to her brass-contained plumpness. Clothe a woman in metal and though it's cold, she is suddenly not just futuristic, but dressing for domination—within a single picture both facets of the sexual male stereotype are catered for. Book covers still show women if not fully naked, then ragged, as if abused in such a way that the secondary sexual characteristics are focussed upon. Doctor Who can run about in overcoat and scarf, but Leela must continually fall over, legs flying and skimpy loin cloth parting to give a hint of backside. Strangely, though, in fantasy fiction, heroic fantasy or sword and sorcery, call it what you will, in this particular sub-genre everyone seems to run about unclothed. All manner of muscle-bound heroes tread the mountains and forests or worlds where magic rules, and women submit readily, and they all share one characteristic—they are super-male, overloaded with Y chromosomes, carrying the symbols of manhood in both hands (and a few in their belts, or on their heads) and speaking the short, gruff, meaning-charged phrases of either a moron or a man who saves his energy for more important things, such as indiscriminate slaughter.

Dare one suggest that these meatheads dress and behave for the benefit of other male barbarians—and male readers—rather than for the mountainously built women they seem so reluctant to bed? Why *did* Conan of Cimmeria become a mercenary? Surely not because he was found in flagrante dilecto with Brak the Barbarian! Who knows. The women will never tell—they rarely have speaking parts, and complete descriptions of them become

Princess Vivianne *The daughter of the Emperor Rothgar V, she became a space pirate at the age of 21 and was renowed on the trade routes of the Star Forest Zone for her bold and fearless attacks on all manner of craft. The Aldebaran 'croot' with her is her space pilot.*

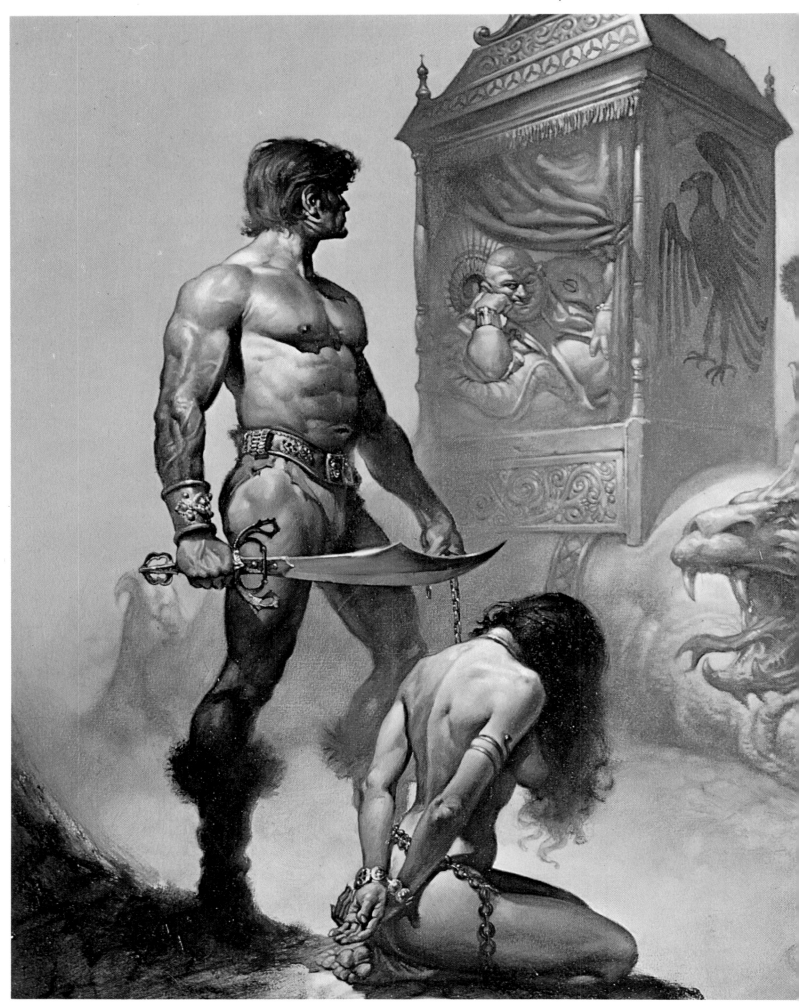

monotonously familiar—all those high, jutting breasts, proud bearings, cascades of flowing red hair, fiery green eyes, full pouting lips, wide hips, gossamer robes clinging to the high points of their bodies . . . and underneath, perhaps, a little something black and leathery? No chance. Fantasy worlds are manly worlds, where the wind blows the stench of blood, and wild beasts prowl the nightmare landscapes, and strong men ride out of the dawn mist on great black stallions, broadswords clutched in hand as easily as a child holds a toffee apple. There are always deeds to be done, money to earn for killing a few people here and there, wizards to conquer, bad kings to overthrow, pouting princesses to service, black mountains and towers with terrible secrets to release. Machismo rules the cardboard landscapes, and though all those jutting breasts and long, hard jaw-lines make the books very hard to close, this is hardly a claim for good characterisation.

Some fantasy heroes and heroines, however, stand out from the fleshpots, usually because their authors are half way competent, or have come up with some original notion with which to equip their prose or character. Conan of Cimmeria is an original, perhaps *the* original, a mercenary wandering the lands around his homeland of Cimmeria (the northern hemisphere of Earth at some distant future time) selling his sword and skills to the various warrior kings scattered around. Conan derives directly from the Rider Haggard noble warrior-type from Africa, a strong and violent man bound nonetheless by his own deep-seated code of behaviour. He is contrasted beautifully by Michael Moorcock's fantasy parody, Elric. Elric is at once everything the fantasy super heroes are made out to be, muscular, strong, stupid, and at the same time an albino dwarf, frantically projecting the super-strong image using his own mental powers. Elric's sword is the famous Stormbringer, which seeks and steals souls with a mind of its own, drinking the warrior spirit of a man as it drinks his blood; at the end of *Stormbringer* itself, the spirit escapes: the entity that was Stormbringer, last manifestation of Chaos which would remain with this new world as it grew, looked down on the corpse of Elric of Melnibone and smiled: 'Farewell, friend. I was a thousand times more evil than thou!'

The continuing battle between Order

Market Killing *Caught by the scimitar-wielding desert trader from the tribe of the Whaterzi on Kettle's World, this female Terran tourist, whose family has been slaughtered, is to be executed herself. She is taken to the 'pleasure route', where fat and slimy city traders come to slaver over the brutal butchery and execution of unwary travellers. This man has paid over 1,000 credits to ogle as the girl is beheaded.*

and Chaos is a common theme in most sword and sorcery novels, even in the so-called higher fantasy, such books as are written by C. S. Lewis, J. R. R. Tolkein and Susan Cooper. Order and Chaos are the two great changing forces in the universe—scientifically they would be known as positive and negative entropy—and all nations, empires and moves to annex neighbouring countries can be seen as reflections of Chaos in the world. Naturally, most super heroes become agents for one or other of the two governing forces. Few, though, are so intimately involved with Chaos as Richard Kirk's *Raven, Swordsmistress of Chaos*, one of the newer fantasy heroines, and unusual in that she is both woman, dominant, violent and romantic, and now commanding a huge readership. Most female characters in fantasy are sex objects, kept that way both in the book and in the reader's mind, and when they do manage a certain individuality—Jane Gaskell's Atlan, for example, or most of Tanith Lee's female protagonists—they tend to be fantastic recreations of the ultra-modern feminist, a woman in body a 'person' in mind and attitude. Raven is all woman, bisexual and enormously happy to indulge her body and the bodies of others. She has been chosen for her role as Swordsmistress of Chaos, plucked from the slavepens of Lyand by the mysterious Sorcerer Priests and schooled in every art of weaponry until no mere man can defeat her—in *any* form of physical combat. And gradually Raven recognises her role in the world, as she consults earth oracles, and speaks with ancient forces below the planet's crust: 'The world turns, Raven, though its spin may end at any point. A brake is required, a pivot point, a place, a being, at which things rest in readiness to be shaped. You, Raven, are that focus. You are the axis of the world. Upon you depends the world.'

Karl Edward Wagner's Kane is a modern version of the fantasy hero who is quite unique, and who many regard as being the best of the modern characters. Kane is an immortal who has been doomed to roam the Earth forever by the god that created him; the punishment has been levelled at Kane because Kane has killed his own brother and thus brought terrible violence to the Earth; the irony is that the god was a corrupt and cynical part of the supernatural universe overruling Earth, and Kane has rebelled against being used as a pawn, while his race is herded about like sheep. His adventures take place in all the ages of Earth, and his sword and battle prowess is at the service of any ruler who can pay his price. Kane's outstanding features are his flame-red hair and beard, and his deep blue eyes, the eyes of a killer—the mark of Cain! He is a true anti-hero who changes sides to suit his own advantage and mood; he never ages and remaining as old as he was when the god cursed him. He can be killed but up to now no human has come close to doing so, although supernatural entities try and almost succeed in every book.

A supernatural entity is the bane of Chris Carlsen's magnificent character The Berserker, a nordic warrior cursed by Odin for disobedience and transformed into one of the wild and inhumanly violent berserkers. He is known as Swiftaxe, but his fate is to die and be reborn in different ages, in different physical manifestations, until he can survive a mortal wound, a paradox that he desperately tries to break. Meanwhile, from life to life the ill-fated Swiftaxe finds himself pitted against the forces of man and the supernatural in different ages from Roman Britain to Arthurian Britain, and from the Ireland of the ancient Celts to Norway of the years of *a-viking*. The refreshing thing about Swiftaxe is that he is by no means a muscular super hero, merely a warrior with totally unpredictable and uncontrollable violence—the author uses him as a symbol, a whirling focus, for the unpredictable and violent social change that was such a dominant feature of the Iron Age. The novels, especially *The Bull Chief*, can be read as historical novels where the supernatural beliefs of the peoples are actually made manifest; as fantasy novels they are in a class apart from routine sword and sorcery, and like Kane have a cult following.

Hothouse *A world where man's terraforming went haywire, the trees and plants growing to enormous sizes and the human colonists reverting to a fairy-like existence, such as this Tree Knight, a forest guardian from one of the tribes.*

Worlds Apart

'. . . the eerie, crystalline landscapes and the bizarre future worlds'

efore you embark on a package tour of the galaxy, it is best to know which worlds are more than just devastatingly beautiful alien landscapes. For every planet where we have gained a footing and held our own, there are two where the hidden alien dangers of the landscape might easily destroy us.

When the Russian spacecraft *Venera* penetrated the sulphurous clouds of Venus a few years ago and landed on a bleak, stony, acid and heat-scarred landscape, a thousand sf hearts sank; gone in a second were the dreams of the lush and deadly rain jungles that had finally killed the lost earthmen in Ray Bradbury's 'The Long Rain'; gone were the vast green islands of weed floating on a surging ocean of C. S. Lewis's *Voyage to Venus*; gone the rocky terrain with its deep mines and underground communities of Fred Pohl's 'Come To Venus Melancholy'; all gone, in the same instant that all hope of ever learning to live upon Venus were dashed as well. With an atmospheric pressure a hundred times greater than Earth's, a cloud density that includes carbon dioxide and sulphuric acid among its heavier components, a surface temperature of 900° centigrade, life as we know it could not possibly survive, or have evolved there.

Strangely, the same fate of disillusionment has not befallen Mars. The most recent notable science fiction dealing with Mars as we now know it, for example William Wallings 'Nix Olympica', makes of the real Mars something as mystic and as exciting as any Mars of romantic literature: and Mars, the sandswept, windswept, cratered world, with its enormous volcanoes and plateaux rising thousands of feet above the deserts, this world is as exciting, as mysterious as anything that Edgar Rice Burroughs or Ray Bradbury, ever imagined.

Which is not to say that the mythical, now romantic Mars, enters an area of dead literature. Far from it. The eerie, crystalline landscape of Bradbury's series of stories *The Martian Chronicles* is surely one of the most memorable alien landscapes in modern sf. Who can forget the sparkle of sun on the ruined, bone-like buildings of the ancient Martian race, buildings scattered on each horizon, and around the sandswept human installations, and the deep canals, drying up now, sheerwalled with crumbling brickwork and decaying metal frames, testifying to the greatness that has gone.

Bradbury's Mars is nothing like the hostile Mars envisioned by H. G. Wells, whose grotesque intelligences peer at the uncrowded green spaces of earth with a planet-sized avarice, and shoot invasion capsules through guns so vast that their flash and fire can be seen from earth. What a dark world Wells painted by implication, a darkness echoed in Nigel Kneale's unforgettable play *Quatermass and the Pit*, where the remains of a Martian craft are discovered in the clays of London; the invading aliens having interfered with the development of prehistoric Englishmen, half the inhabitants of these islands now have a racial memory of the overcrowded world of the insect-like Martians, and the terrible, devastating pressures that have caused their invasion. Dark worlds indeed, and violent, yet none so violent as Edgar

Alien City of Bash'kaz *The Faberian city located on snow world Draco 7, a large, heavy gravity planet (5G) with an indigenous semi-intelligent life form. By agreement with the Terran Federation, colonisation has not expanded beyond this single installation.*

Valley of the Statues *A strange feature of the planet Ree'hdworld is this high mountain valley filled with fragmented and alien carvings. The world has two indigenous life forms, the intelligent burrow-living Ree'hd, and a semi-intelligent related species the Rundii. The world's most notable feature is the incredible wind—the Earth wind—that blows about it in advance of the terminator.*

Moon', an alien egg cracks open to release an invisible terror that seems to want to eat the Terran dome itself. In James Blish's memorable story 'Bridge', engineers fight the relentless methane storms in Jupiter to try and build a bridge out of Ice IV.

The planet Mercury turns on its axis. With the revelation of this discovery a hundred stories about the tiny world become exercises in fantasy; and most notable to go, perhaps, Isaac Asimov's robot story 'Reason'. However, the cratered, boiling/freezing world now becomes a challenge to artist and writer alike, stretching the imagination to find ways of exploiting its environmental violence to the ends of science fiction.

Arthur Clarke has had fun with the satellites of the great planets, though little of the landscape of Iapetus (*2001: A Space Odyssey*) remains in memory as he sends the astronaut Bowman, through a gigantic alien structure on this tiny, barren world, a building that is the start of a star gate that allows Bowman to journey across the universe. The landscape of Titan, one of the largest satellites of Saturn, is more vividly imagined in *Imperial Earth*; Clarke describes it as a red world, where the red hue—Mars-like, angry— is caused by the same organic mix in the lower atmosphere as causes the famous Jovian red spot. The atmosphere of Titan, being dense, can cause a hothouse effect, and in places the surface temperature—despite the distance of the sun—is tremendously high, and the heat creates as many problems as the more usual bitter cold. Titan is covered by wide, shallow ammonia lakes, in which fantastically shaped bergs and floes of ammonia-ice float, but the slightest warm breeze can cause the lakes to flash evaporate, creating hellish 'methane monsoons' and generating blasting, 300 mph winds, which devastate the flimsy terrestrial structures.

It seems strange that although the imaginative intensity and creative ability of science fiction writers and artists has made the field a jungle of ideas and bizarre future worlds, for many people the most memorable sf world is a desert wasteland. Dune, known more properly as Arrakis, has featured in several novels by Frank Herbert, of which the best is the first, *Dune* itself. The vision of the world was born from an assignment to Oregon to write about the US Agricultural De-

Rice Burrough's vision of a Mars populated by beasts and warlike races, all strongly reminiscent of African and South American tribes. Burroughs is the true romantic, the Rider Haggard of the solar system, sending his intrepid hero on all manner of adventures, meeting princesses and princes of the Red Planet, and generally surviving against all odds. Barsoom, as it is known to the inhabitants, is a dying world of forests bordered by vast red deserts, and peopled by three Martian races, the green, the red and the white Martians, and white Martian princesses have to be seen to be believed.

Elsewhere in the solar system the planets orbit and await the approach of bigger and better probes to elucidate their true secrets; meanwhile the art and the fiction continues, their fantastic futures remain intact, and the moons of Jupiter and Saturn continue to function as sites for some splendid and vivid science fiction, notably at the hands of Arthur Clarke. Triton, a moon of Neptune, houses Samuel Delany's hostile society beneath its perspex dome in the most violent and difficult of his novels, *Triton*; on the desolate rock and dust strewn landscape of Luna in Paul Ernst's 'Nothing Ever Happens On The

partment's attempts to control sand dunes, plus the author's growing belief that messiahs are the creation of men unable to cope with their own social responsibilities. In four novels, *Duneworld*, *Prophet of Dune*, *Dune Messiah* and *Children of Dune*, Frank Herbert has traced the history of this remarkable world, and the Atreides family and their continuing struggle to retain control against more mercenary and violent forces, not the least of which is the planet Arrakis itself.

Arrakis is a world so dry, so heat and wind scoured, that every drop of moisture is precious, and therefore hoarded; moisture is wealth, and with no open body of water on the world, it is sought almost as desperately as is the spice *melange*. The cities are only in the north, protected from the terrible sandblast storms by walls or deep basins, and the mountains called Shield Wall; but not all the human population lives here. In the central desert, which is a land of killer storms and the gigantic sandworms that can swallow whole machines unnoticed, there live Freman raiders, inhabiting warrens of caves in the sterile hills. All Arrakian activity centres around the mining of *melange* from the sandworm-guarded deserts, for *melange* can increase mental power

in so many ways that it is one of the most precious materials in the universe, and a source of indefinite wealth to those who control it.

Several artists have tackled the task of conveying the wonderland of rock and sand that is this amazing world, but none have succeeded as brilliantly as John Schoenherr, who illustrated the original serials in *Analog*; his vision of the towering, bizarre, sculpted pinnacles of rock, the complexities of caves and gullies, whose hollow echoing almost resounds from the painting itself, and the drum wastes of desert where the slightest footfall echoes so loud it risks calling the sandworms to the surface, is surely definitive; Schoenherr's pictures speak for Arrakis as Herbert speaks for the intrigue and politicking that goes on upon the land world itself.

The image of a sandworld may seem bland at first glance, but Arrakis is remarkable and it is not the only desert landscape to feature in science fiction. Most notable in the fiction is probably Cordwainer Smith's 'On The Sand Planet'; and Tattooine, from Star Wars, springs to mind as a cinematographic desert world; it is more memorable than the red deserts of Forbidden Planet, on which a marooned Earthman has

learned to live with and among the enormous ruins and still-functioning energy machines of a dead alien race. The vision of Tattooine is of a Dune-like world across which enormous machines roam, gathering metal waste, and within and upon which live scattered alien and human tribes, all adapted to the heat and sterility of the desert.

What a total contrast is Harry Harrison's *Deathworld*. The planet Pyrrus is surely the most traditionally violent world ever to be described in science fiction, not so much from the climatic point of view, but totally. Every plant and animal on Pyrrus is a killer, and the whole planet is a jungle, a deadly place for any man without lightning reflexes and eyes in the back of his head. Plants with teeth, armour-plated animals, things that fly, swoop, burrow or just charge through the jungle, attacking with razor claws and gleaming fangs; they have, in fact, reacted to innate human violence, sensing it telepathically, and now survive by matching anger with anger, fear with fear, protectiveness with protectiveness.

Different again is Hal Clement's Mesklin; there is nothing particularly dangerous on this world as far as life forms are concerned; but like Arrakis the physical and climatic environment is daunting in its violence. Mesklin is a truly memorable world, and all credit to Clement for conceiving of a planet shaped not like a ball, but like a discus. Mesklin spins horizontally, and naturally enough the edge of the disc is spinning many times faster than the centre, and the centrifugal forces there are staggering, not to mention the winds, storms and other physical effects

of a hugely increased gravitational field. Only the native inhabitants of Mesklin, charming centipedal creatures, can make the journey to the edge of the world to pick up a human probe that has crashed there, and their journey is the subject of *Mission of Gravity*. Mesklinites are hired in *Star Light* to explore Dhrawn, a planet with a gravity 40 times higher than Earth because it is, in fact, a star/planet companion to a red dwarf sun. In terms of mass, it is halfway between Jupiter and the red dwarf itself but it is devoid of any light elements, which is confusing the exploring terrestrial cosmologists. Dhrawn generates internal heat, and though it is mainly cold, it has regions as hot as 1200° Kelvin. There is oxygen around, and water/ammonia oceans that give off vast and lingering ammonia fogs, making the Mesklinites' journey hazardous and exciting. Kelly Freas has

LEFT
Privateer near one of Saturn's Moons *Thought to be a part of the immense Laker empire, a mining, transport and armaments company that developed over several centuries from the Earth-based empire of a trillionaire recluse, this privateer and its luxury moon base is typical of the private yachts and solar shuttles that were based on the barren 'free zone' asteroids throughout the 21st and 22nd centuries.*

BELOW
Ferryport, Trantor *Trantor was the administrative centre of the Great Empire, and was a world totally covered by steel. The original city is thought to have been quite small, but it expanded so rapidly, as so many new worlds came under the protection of the early Federation, that it soon extended beyond all horizons until it practically covered the world's surface. The ferryports were giant mini-cities (mini-scapes) built above the skin of the world.*

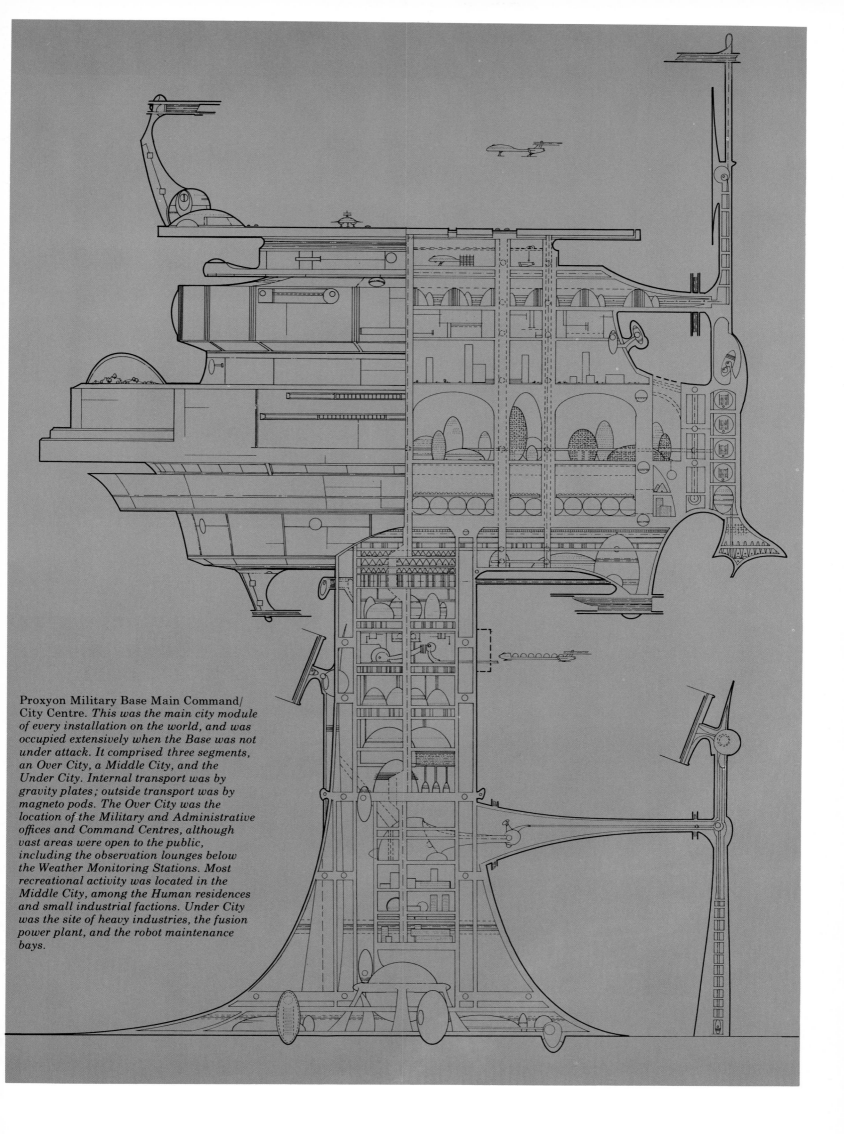

Proxyon Military Base Main Command/
City Centre. *This was the main city module
of every installation on the world, and was
occupied extensively when the Base was not
under attack. It comprised three segments,
an Over City, a Middle City, and the
Under City. Internal transport was by
gravity plates; outside transport was by
magneto pods. The Over City was the
location of the Military and Administrative
offices and Command Centres, although
vast areas were open to the public,
including the observation lounges below
the Weather Monitoring Stations. Most
recreational activity was located in the
Middle City, among the Human residences
and small industrial factions. Under City
was the site of heavy industries, the fusion
power plant, and the robot maintenance
bays.*

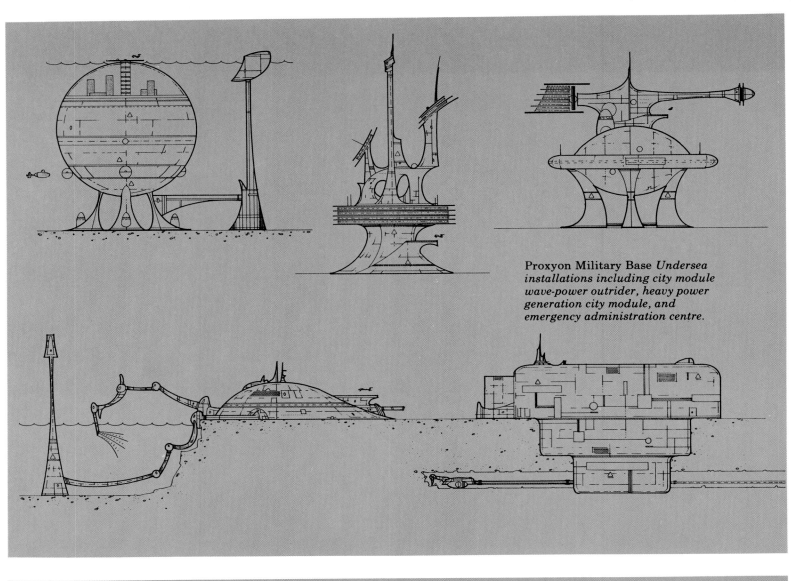

Proxyon Military Base *Undersea installations including city module wave-power outrider, heavy power generation city module, and emergency administration centre.*

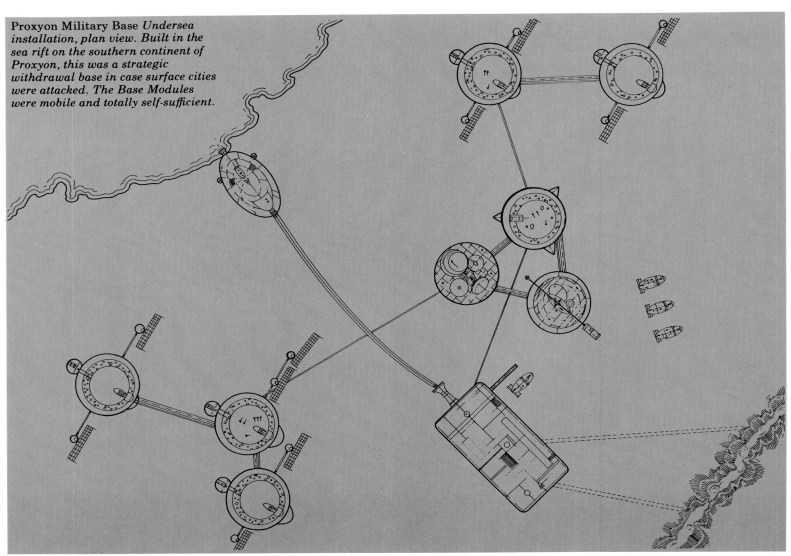

Proxyon Military Base *Undersea installation, plan view. Built in the sea rift on the southern continent of Proxyon, this was a strategic withdrawal base in case surface cities were attacked. The Base Modules were mobile and totally self-sufficient.*

New Milford *The ghostly image of a Faberian crystal ship hovers above the northern hemisphere of the contested world of New Milford. The atmosphere on New Milford is thin, more suitable to Faberian colonisation than Human, but during the Interregnum, New Milford's mineral wealth was realised, especially the so-called 'wisdom nuggets', crystals of carbon silicon alloy that are useful in information recording and retrieval systems. Eventually five Terran installations were set up, each protected by an orbiting military base: Mariannas-ville, Charlottaville, Redd City, Garnett's Haven, and Brunner Base.*

Peyton City *The book market of the galaxy, Peyton City was built on the planet Andromeda in the Alpha Cruxus system, known as Summer Row because of the five Earth-type worlds that orbit this G-type sun at comfortable distances. The whole system is an enormous tourist attraction, and possibly the richest non-mineral system in the galaxy. Andromeda, the most distant of the worlds, has 40 market cities, all connected by vac-tubes to facilitate swift visiting. The book city is estimated to stock over 400 million individual items of Terran, Faberian and other alien literature. The city is named after the man who built the original shanty town, a mysterious figure from history known both as the Rocking Roller, because of his crippled gait, and as the Barbarian, perhaps the same Emperior Barbus who was drowned in a vat of Centaurian mead.*

illustrated the world, as he illustrated Mesklin, and has managed to capture much of the alienness of the place.

Not all alien worlds are memorable for their natural strangeness. In Isaac Asimov's classic trilogy *Foundation*, the central world of the Imperial Government is the memorably horrifying planet of Trantor; although the search for the mysterious Second Foundation takes a bevy of heroes across the length and breadth of the spiral galaxy, it is Trantor, the totally concrete and metal covered starting point of the search that lives in memory. All the land surface of Trantor, 75 million square miles, is a single city, its human population well in excess of 40 billion; each day tens of thousands of ships bring agricultural supplies to the massive urban centre, whose work force is part of the most densely populated and industrially advanced world in the galaxy. Gaal Dornick documents his first impression of Trantor:

'He could not see the ground. It was lost in the ever-increasing complexities of man-made structures. He could see no horizon other than that of metal against sky, stretching out to almost uniform greyness, and he knew it was all over the land surface surface of the planet'.

Trantor, never effectively painted itself, is surely reflected in Blair Wilkins' magnificent paintings.

But the fate of Trantor is a foregone conclusion in a galactic empire that is so large it is impossible to control opposite ends of it at the same time. Inevitably parts of the empire are neglected, and rise in revolt, and Trantor increasingly becomes the central focus of their attacks, for on Trantor is the administrative heart of the empire, housed and attended to by all who live in the metal skin. The empires fall, and with them the populated worlds, especially the rich and affluent worlds. Trantor is not rich, but it is vital to the control of the empire, and soon it is attacked, devasted and left a wasteland. The farmers return, and the metal skin is stripped away and sold for agricultural wares. After thousands of years a grey metallic jewel in the galaxy, Trantor has become a ruined world, with sprawling farms reaching around the shards and twisted metal remnants of the planet-wide city.

Ruined worlds hold a fascination for science fiction, and many stories have been written featuring exploration teams who find a planet covered with the rusting buildings, shattered domes and enigmatic hieroglyphs of a vanished race, and must try and piece together the nature of the glory that was. Sometimes towering buildings contain a treasurehouse of knowledge that will take mankind an eternity to translate and interpret, as in Robert Heinlein's 'Jackpot'; sometimes the scattered ruins of statues and cities contain a grim warning for our future, as in Robert Silverberg's 'Ozymandius' where the aliens' own inability to cope with power has reduced their world to rubble. Sometimes, as in Clifford Simak's 'Limiting Factor', an entire ruined world, Trantor-like in that its skin is totally of steel now, defies mankinds most energetic attempts to comprehend that which has been left for him to find.

Science fiction has described, and

Platt City *One of the ugliest cities in the Old Empire, Platt City grew from a small shanty town on Laodbrokke's World, a haven for social dropouts, drug addicts, the deformed, the feeble-minded, and a huge number of artists and writers among whom were many brilliant literary expositors. The city was named after one of the least talented writers, whose immense boys' adventure* Garbage Galaxy *was nevertheless popular throughout the system and financed the construction of this steel city.*

written about, literally thousands of alien worlds, and a recurrent theme is the Earth-type world, where something is devastatingly alien, but unnoticed. In the visual media, especially *Star Trek*, the universe would appear to consist of nothing but Earth-type worlds, even if a few flowers have been turned upside down in a token attempt to give some other-worldliness to the place. This sort of cop-out abounds in the written form, but more often than not is used to point out the danger of familiarity. Many writers conveniently point out the fact of the planet's earlier 'terraforming' (making earth-like), while others spend a chapter in which the characters react with considerable shock to the 'staggering odds' against another such a world actually existing in the universe.

But where the point of the science fiction is the fiction and not the science, the Earth-type world comes into its own as a sinister and memorable place. Bradbury is especially good at exploiting the lurking alienness in an otherwise totally familiar scene. In his short story 'The City', for example, he describes an Earth-type world and a deserted alien city that is possessed of an ancient, but lingering, machine intelligence. It captures, dissects and re-uses a human exploration team who have lost their guard.

The snow wastes on Ursula K. Le Guin's winter world, Gethan, in *The Left Hand of Darkness* seem familiar enough to begin with, but rapidly become as alien as the hermaphroditic peoples who live there. Stanislaw Lem's *Solaris*, as a landscape, is monotonously familiar . . . a single, planet-wide ocean, with strange wave patterns and currents and bizarre surface formations, mostly concealed beneath drifting clouds: but solaris has a secret that ultimately destroys the Terran expedition there, for the ocean is a single gigantic organism.

Many worlds have been converted into prisons, James White's *Open Prison*, for example, but most seem only too terrestrial compared to Cordwainer Smith's *A Planet named Shayol*, where the landscape is of sand and rock, arid and deserted save for the fragments of horrifyingly mutated human beings who live there, almost growing out of the ground itself.

Not all alien landscapes are alien worlds, the setting for some fantastic futures are alien *things*. Following hard on the heels of Freeman Dyson's

ideas of a gigantic, artificial world built as a ring or sphere of metal around a sun, came two novels both of which mind-bendingly explored the possibilities of such worlds.

Larry Niven's Ringworld has a metal base and millions of square miles of rock, earth, plants, air and mountain ecology built upon the inner surface of a 180 million mile diameter band of metal, spinning about the sun. Night and day are ordered by the movement of Shadow Squares, orbiting between the sun and the gigantic metal ring. It is an enigmatic alien artefact, deserted by the aliens who built it; but why they built it is obvious, for it has an enormous agricultural surface area.

The Dyson Sphere was itself explored in Bob Shaw's *Orbitsville*. The land surface of the sphere is an ordinary planetary distance from the sun, but the sun is totally enclosed by the artificial metal world, whose interior surface is a grassy, rocky landscape, trillions of square miles in extent. It takes years, flying at supersonic speed, to return to the sprawling city around

Garnett's Haven *One of the earliest cities on New Milford, Garnett's Haven was built in the southern hemisphere in the area known as Black Rock. The city was allowed to fall into some disrepair, but eventually picked itself up and became one of the brightest and most active cities on New Milford. Population at the end of the Second Empire was only two million, small for a popular base such as this.*

the split in the shell that is the way in. The orbitsville is so vast that entire alien cultures have been established on its surface, separated by such astronomical distance from other cultures that it will be generations before they can ever meet and mingle.

Such grandiose concepts stretch the talents of even the most imaginative of writers, and yet what imagination there is too at the opposite end of the scale. The smallest world ever envisaged sensibly in sf is in James Blish's *Surface Tension*, in which human colonists are engaged in a life and death struggle against their watery world as it shrinks and threatens to crush them by surface tension alone—they have been genetically bred as minute creatures and inhabit a puddle on an otherwise hostile world! Decades before this, G. Peyton Wertenbaker had written his stories about the man from the atom, in which a scientist is first shrunk so much that he can see how all the electrons orbiting the protons of atoms are just planetary systems like our own; when the reverse occurs and he enlarges to fantastic proportions he naturally discovers that our own solar system is just an atom in some gigantic alien coffee table.

Gateway is an alien construct, based on an asteroid, described by Frederik Pohl in his recent award-winning novel. It is, in fact, a transgalactic dispatching point complete with automatic pilot vessels. Earthmen risk their lives in these alien gadgets, never knowing whether they will be transmitted to Earth's moon, or into intergalactic space. In Bradbury's 'Perchance To Dream' a marooned spaceman sits on the barren, rocky waste of a tiny asteroid, watching the black of space and the brilliance of the stars, hoping for some sign of rescue. When rescue arrives however, it is too late to save him from possession by the ghosts of the people who had lived here, millennia before, when the asteroid cluster had been a single, vast and lush planet. Harry Harrison's world in *Captive Universe* at first appears to be a valley, surrounded and cut off by high mountains, a valley guarded by the violent goddess Coatlico, who punishes all attempts to escape the valley; legend tells of the sun running across the sky each day on trackways, which seems nonsensical until you realise that this world is a generation ship built within an asteroid, and the sun really *does* run on tracks!

Generation ships are an important part of sf's view of man's fantastic future, and of course such gigantic vessels, travelling for thousands of years between the stars in search of new worlds, are in one sense alien landscapes, and are often very memorable as such.

In Brian Aldiss's *Nonstop* the hydroponic farms that were designed to supply food for the generations-long trip have grown out of control so that the ship becomes a jungle, and different decks are cut off from each other. Each develops its own tribal groups, and laws, and rituals. James Blish's *Cities in Flight* appear to be ordinary futuristic city-scapes, tower blocks and sky-scrapers, roads and skyways, all covered by a vast, translucent dome; but though the city is still attached to the ground and bedrock on which it was built, all that rock has been lifted from the Earth on giant anti-gravity engines and is now skimming between solar systems; the city states have become space traders in their own right.

Finally there is the fantastic future of our planet, and the imaginations of science fiction writers have seen the future Earth as a very alien and fantastic place indeed. Perhaps the earliest such vision that is memorable is H. G. Wells' conception of the very end of the world itself, a dark place, eerily lit by the now dim and very red Sun; the time traveller from Wells' magnificent story 'The Time Machine' emerges onto a darkened beach, close to the sluggish, stagnant ocean, no longer drawn up in

tides or waves since the Moon has long
since crashed to the earth. Giant crabs
and enormous, white butterfly-like
creatures are all he glimpses before the
panic of this long dead place sends him
back to Victorian London.

Isaac Asimov's vision of future Earth,
as typified in *The Caves of Steel*, is of a
planet where everyone has gone underground, into vast, steel-lined caves,
from which they fear to emerge because
of the wide-open agricultural areas,
and the terror of space and hidden
danger. A similar vision, far nastier,
far more pertinent, is E. M. Forster's
conception of a world of battery humans
in 'The Machine Stops'; here, everyone
lives in a beehive-like cell below the
ground, nourished by the machine that
is the city; they are fearful of the deadly
radioactive wastelands above them,
wastelands that have long since returned to nature.

Robert Silverberg played cruel tricks
with time and the unpredestined nature
of man when he took his party-goers
forward to the bitter end of time in
'When We Went To See The End Of The
World'; each man who takes the trip,
and sees the ruined, empty earth, sees
a different ruined and empty earth from
anyone else—some see parched deserts,

others forest wildernesses, others radioactive wastelands, and most memorable
of all, one sees a snow and ice covered
world, with the ruins of skyscrapers
towering out of the glaciers, and buildings fast crumbling before the onslaught of the Ice Age.

In the future too, sf has seen human
change running parallel with, even
symbolised by, environmental change.
The classic novels of J. G. Ballard all
depict bizarre earthscapes, and the
human characters in them assume the
environment like some bizarre inner
layer of clothing: crystalline landscape,
in *The Crystal World*, aglitter with
jewels, where plants and animals have
facets, now, and jungles shimmer like
diamonds; or *The Drowned World*,
where everywhere is tropical, flooded,
lush; or perhaps most memorable of
all, the *Vermilion Sands*, in which the
red sands that have drifted everywhere,
in and out of the ruined shells of man's
deserted estates. Ballard is one of the
most accomplished creators of evoca-
tive landscapes in modern science fiction, Daliesque certainly, mixing the
familiar and the exotic, making an
artform of decay and degeneration,
making the future truly fantastic and
stretching imagination to the limit.

Glossary

Ames Drive: conventional drive mechanism of all First and Second Federation war and passenger ships—direct borinium 'shatter' power and quark regeneration fine matter/antimatter hostile phase interference power combine in the Ames drive to make it the most efficient ship drive ever devised.

Carlsen 20 cm Split Beam Violator: one of the most unusual weapons fitted to warships, the C20SV was shaped like an axehead and drew on the electric body-power of the 'gunner'—it was unstable in fierce battle and had a habit of fatally de-electrifying the operator.

C-holding Factor: gravity wave and spontaneous space-flux and distortion make it difficult for a ship travelling at super light speeds to maintain a constant s-t velocity—a balance between Einvelocity and Ziemen fluctuation ability, plus mass, time and intrinsic radiated energy give the C-holding factor.

Duralium Shield: protective hull shield for warships, created by time-phase interference of Duralium subatomic decay.

Einvelocity: accepted measure of relative space-time velocity at light-fabric-distortion power. After Lunan-modified Einsteinian relativity.

Elerac: major arms industry of Independent Worlds—factories mainly built on lifeless world of Weston's Fall.

Jackson's Rift: planetary feature of Algol 3, a rift over four miles deep and two hundred miles long, used in the latter part of the Zone Wars as a combat ground.

Matter Regeneration Capability: fitted to ships on long thru space journeys, the MR capacity was a function of the matter/antimatter balance in the ship's drive, and was a way of delaying the build up of antimatter to the critical point by use of quark duplication.

Pin Mines: explosive microdots of antimatter, contained in a life-activated-decay metal shell and grav-distortion phase field. Used during all wars to seed enemy battle zones.

Proxyon III: Terran planet, devoid of natural life, but with otherwise very Earth-type atmosphere and geology, including several deep oceans and water filled rifts. Made into military base, with four hundred separate military/civilian installations.

Rundii: Galactic enigma, the Rundii are semi-intelligent creatures living in mountain and forest zones of the planet Ree'hdworld; main life form on Ree'hdworld are the Ree'hd themselves, who are burrow dwellers, but whose legends tell of a technologically advanced race that had once lived here thousands of years before.

Spindizzy: anti-gravity engines, first used to lift entire cities from Earth, later used as emergency lifts for colonial complexes on hostile or contested worlds.

Synhominoids: Robot class, usually weapon or personal bodyguard, styled in human form and with organic emplacements, usually neuro-muscular, enabling fine control of movement.

Thru Space Life: such fundamental 'space proximity' distortion as enables a ship to pass thru space has a negative effect on the ship's mass, converting micro-particle to antimatter at a steady rate—when more than 1% of the micro-particles are in this state the ship becomes unstable.

Trantor: colonised world completely covered with metal and buildings. Became administrative centre of the Galaxy, but was vulnerable to attack and was finally destroyed during Second Empire.

Wingrove Rapid Fatigue Weapons Systems: carried by most Federation vessels in one form or another, this historic weapons system supplied intense fire power on many phase levels for a short period of time. Of use in swift attacks, it was superseded for more prolonged battle by the Harvey wide-bore mega-joint weapons system.

Ziemen: unit measure of matter-energy-space interaction at high velocity—proportional to time displacement so can be critical. Some hull-energy fields give greater displacement without increasing time.

Federations

During the third to the fifth millennia inclusive, three different Federations were formed from the disparate Terran worlds of the Galaxy, each one characterised by a different 'Free Zone' (free trade exploitable planetary systems), a different frontier zone with the various alien inhabitants of the star city, and also by the differing centre of rule; at some time during each Federation period a Terran Empire was declared, and the periods between these Empires are known, conveniently, as the Interregnums. The Empires, with their first rulers, were as follows:

First Empire, declared by Jaar K'rath Mellows, a Terran, founded and based on Earth, and lasting 530 years.

Second Empire, declared by Kriston Abel Farenzio, a Bootian trader and politician, founded on Vega, but with strong ties with Earth, and lasting 400 years.

Third Empire, declared by Birikoff Brishoff macSuriyamana, a nomad and religious leader of some note; the Third Empire began on Vega but when this declared itself an Independent Principality—peace was declared over this issue after the Second Ursan Convention—the focus of the Empire moved first to the artificial world Mechanistra, and thence back to the Solar Worlds, mainly Mars.

Zone Wars

The collective name for 14 territorial space wars fought between the end of the fifth millennium and throughout the sixth; mainly intra-Terran squabbles, several Zone Wars involved alien races, notably the Faberians who by the time of the sixth Zone War had vested interested in a number of Federation (Empire) worlds. The entire Zone Wars lasted only a total of 70 years.

Final War: fought mainly in the Tucana M system, and using Mechanistra and other artificial satellite worlds with immense fire-capability, the Final War lasted a mere ten Earth years, but was the most fiercely fought of the 14 Zone Wars; it began as a small industrial worlds' dispute, but became the battle zone for wider issues between Human and the Faberian-assisted Sarosian Empire.

Thangan War: fought on and in the space around worlds of the Lyran system, the issue with the Thangan Empire, a small alien intrusion into Empire Space, was over their desire to transform their colony worlds in order to correct them environmentally. The Third Empire took issue—despite its surreptitious habit of terra-forming hostile worlds in its own space—and defeated the Thangans in four lengthy, tragic and extremely profitable—to the victors—confrontations.

Nimian War: is now believed to have been a confrontation with these ostensibly peaceful aliens over their progress in time research. The Empire, fearful of the consequences of not breaching time themselves, attacked colony worlds in Nimian space and effectively eradicated the threat. The Empire claimed that three Terran worlds had been obliterated by a Nimian star fleet, and that attacks on Nimian worlds were reprisals; it is now thought that the Terran worlds were destroyed by the Empire itself using captured Nimian vessels.

Time Crashing: occurrence common during the Nimian War, time crashing was caused by overloading of the time-displacement fields with resultant pitching of the ship or machine into Othertime. With the full development of a time-view capability the debris and wreckage so thrown through the time void was monitored and logged and any consequences effectively smoothed and eradicated by the process of 'time reaching'.

Stargates: breaches in the fabric of space, usually associated with a natural gravity sink, and sometimes with the forced distortion of space fields by high-energy thru space distortion and time-space effects. Most Stargates are now logged and known and guarded by Terran-Faberian peace forces. Some Stargates lead out into the universe and are still being explored.

Index

Acknowledgments

The publishers wish to thank the following individuals and organizations for their kind permission to reproduce the pictures in this book:

David Bergen (Ace Books) 73; Sarah Brown Agency (Peter Elson) 59; Vincent Di Fate (Analog) 20, 23, (Berkeley Books) 1; Emsh 45 above; Folio (Melvyn) 13, 38, 40 below, 57, 72 below, (Joe Petagno) 41, 58 above and below; Chris Foss 30 below left; Frank Kelly Freas endpapers, 22, 64 above; David Hardy 60 below, 64–65; Peter Jones 34–35; New English Library (Tim White) 10–11, 53, 69; Rodney Matthews (Big 'O' Publishing) 77; Robert T. McCall 26–27, 33 above and below, 93; Chris Moore 8–9, 14–15, 16–17, 36–37, 52; Tony Roberts (Transworld) 4–5; Thomas Schlück (© David Hardy) *Journey to the Trifid Nebula from Challenge of the Stars* 1972 31 above, *Shooting Star* 1978 49, (© Eddie Jones) cover for TERRA ASTRA No. 269. 1976 6–7, *Star Trek New Voyages* 18, *Star Trek* 19, *Vortex 6* 30 above, *Orion 64* 42 above, *Total Eclipse* 43 below, *Nova 11* 84 above, *Nova 1* 89, (© Paul Lehr) *The Best SF Stories from New Worlds 6* 43 above, *You Will Never Be the Same* 87 below, (Franco Storchi © Editrice Nord) *Untitled* 16, *Untitled* 27, *Untitled* 38–39, *Untitled* 47, (© Michael Whelan) *Armageddon* 50–51, *Chameleon* 62, *The Night Face* 63, *The Vanishing Tower* 68–69, *Gate of Ivrel* 71, *Burial* 72 above, *Outbound* 82, (© Edward Blair Wilkins) *Astarte* 12, *Spindizzies* 25 right, Centre of *Pioneer Triptych* 31 below, *Tigress 11 Docking* 45 below, *Supplying L5* 83, *Perimeter Towers* 84 below, *Roboid No. 3* 91, *Copernicus City* 92; John Schoenherr 42 below, 65 above, 78–79, 90 below; Boris Vallejo (Ballantine Books) 48, 74–75; Young Artists (Jim Burns) 66–67, (Richard Clifton-Dey) 70, (Peter Goodfellow) 81, (Colin Hay) 80, 90 above, (Bob Layzell) 46 below, (Angus McKie) 39, 46 above, 54–55, 87 above, (Terry Oakes) 54–55, 60 above, (Tony Roberts) 44, 56, 88; Gerry Webb of Science Fiction Consultants (photography by Peter Hobbs) 40 above, 61; Patrick Woodroffe 2–3, 24–25.
Illustrations by Roger Full, pages 29, 32, 41 (top right) and Lee Noel, 21, 41 (left), 85, 86.

Our particular thanks are due to: Viv Croot, Ray Hayden and Ernest Hassler.

PDO 79-287